FOREST
PEOPLE
AND
PLACES

To Sheila
With best wishes

Bob Smyth

November 1999

FOREST PEOPLE AND PLACES

BOB SMYTH

PHOTOGRAPHS BY
STEVE CASSIDY

SUTTON PUBLISHING

First published in 1998 by
Sutton Publishing Limited · Phoenix Mill
Thrupp · Stroud · Gloucestershire · GL5 2BU

British Library Cataloguing in Publication Data
A catalogue record for this book is available from the British Library

ISBN 0 7509 1933 7

For CSS

 ALAN SUTTON™ and SUTTON™ are the trade marks of Sutton Publishing Limited

Typeset in 11/12 pt Ehrhardt.
Typesetting and origination by
Sutton Publishing Limited.
Printed in Great Britain by
Ebenezer Baylis, Worcester.

Contents

Introduction and Acknowledgements   ix

1   *Foresters*   1
    John Everard, Deputy Surveyor
    George Aston, woodman
    Brian Mahony, Deputy Surveyor
    Eric Pritchard, wildlife ranger
    Ivan Proctor, RSPB warden

2   *Miners*   9
    Robin Morgan, Hopewell Colliery
    Albert Howell, Deputy Gaveller
    Ray Wright, Clearwell Caves
    Roy Piggott, Deputy Gaveller
    John Harvey, Deputy Gaveller
    Ernest Davies, Waterloo Colliery

3   *Landscapes*   17
    Ray Prosser, Lower Perrygrove Farm
    Ron Aldridge, Lydney District Farmers
    Captain Bill Swinley RN, Haylings Farm
    George and Lynn Woodward, water bailiffs
    Tim Oakes, coracle builder
    Frank and Margaret Baber, Green Cottage
    April and John Tremlett, Millend House

4   *Health*   30
    Dr Arthur Hooper, Drybrook
    Melville Watts, Lydney Hospital
    Professor John Emery, Aylburton
    George and Sue Gordon-Smith, The Orchards

5   *Transport*   35
    Mike Rees, Coleford Railway Museum
    Dougie and Geoff Phelps, and Phil Davies, Norchard Steam Centre

Bill Parker, the Flour Mill
David Evans and Sarah Finch, Dean Heritage Centre
The Grindle family, Grindles coaches

6   *Shopkeepers*   46
Pat Bolter, barber
Keith Morgan, barber
Revd Gordon Johnson, Voluntary Social Service
Doug McLean, bookseller
Phyllis Lewis, sculptor

7   *Church and Chapel*   56
Revd David Addison, Newland C of E
Revd Cliff Davies, Ruardean C of E
Revd Pat Pinkerton, St Briavels C of E
Revd Derek Balsdon, Cinderford Methodists
Revds Andrew and Sally Willett, Littledean United Reformed

8   *Music*   65
Des Yeates, Lydney brass band
Cecil Chappell, Cinderford brass band
Robert Morgan, Lydbrook brass band
Robert Walkerdine, Forest of Dean Male Voice Choir
Hubert Evans, Drybrook Male Voice Choir
Maurice Bent, Ruardean organist
Gill and Wally Marfell, Dean Organ Museum

9   *Writers*   74
Bernard Kear
Joyce Latham
Humphrey Phelps
Andrew Taylor

10   *Historians*   82
Ralph Anstis
Dr Cyril Hart
Brian Johns
Dr Nicholas Herbert

11   *Mansions and Dynasties*   90
St Briavels Castle
Lydney Park
Littledean Hall
Clearwell Castle
Blaisdon Hall

12   *Hotels, Public Houses and Affrays*   101
     Speech House
     Angel Hotel, Coleford
     The Belfry, Littledean
     Royal Foresters, Littledean Hill
     Malt Shovel, Ruardean

Selected Further Reading   114

Index   116

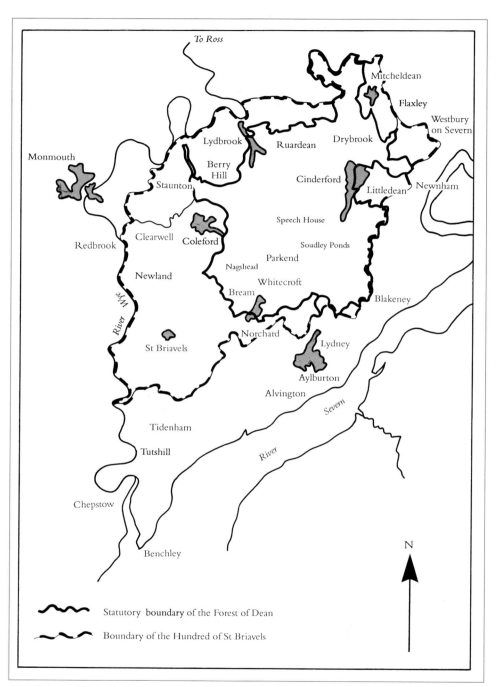

To Ross

Mitcheldean

Flaxley

Westbury
on Severn

Lydbrook   Ruardean   Drybrook

Monmouth

Berry
Hill

Cinderford

Newnham

Staunton

Littledean

Speech House

Clearwell   Coleford

Soudley Ponds

Redbrook

Parkend

Nagshead

Newland

Whitecroft

Bream

Blakeney

River Wye

Norchard

St Briavels

Lydney

Aylburton

Alvington

Severn

Tidenham

Tutshill

River

Chepstow

Benchley

N

〜〜〜 Statutory **boundary** of the Forest of Dean

〜〜〜 Boundary of the Hundred of St Briavels

The Forest of Dean and Hundred of St Briavels.

Introduction and Acknowledgements

When the Revd Henry Nicholls, vicar of Drybrook's Holy Trinity church, published his *The Forest of Dean: An Historical and Descriptive Account* in 1858, he pioneered a tradition of local historians within the Dean which still flourishes today. 'Disappointment expressed by others and felt by myself that a history of the Forest of Dean should never have appeared in print . . . have induced me to attempt its compilation,' he explains in his Preface. No comprehensive single volume history of the Forest has been written in the 140 years since then, but almost every aspect of its forestry and industrial past has been researched by an array of enthusiasts whose achievement is probably unequalled in any other part of Britain.

Supporting their efforts has been a host of archaeologists, researchers, archivists and practical conservationists. The Clearwell Caves iron mines and Hopewell freeminers' drift mine are both open to visitors. Monuments to the Forest's iron industry have been preserved at the Gunn's Mill furnace, the towering Whitecliff furnace, Parkend engine house and Darkhill ironworks. Little remains above ground of the once intensive coal industry apart from Lightmoor's great stone pump house; the coalmasters' mansions at Trafalgar colliery, Cinderford's St Annals House and Drybrook's Euroclydon; Bream's Flour Mill colliery power house; and the brick bath houses of this century's deep pits at Cannop, Whitecroft's Princess Royal and Eastern United at Ruspidge. Of the once extensive tramway and steam railway network, a working section between Norchard and Lydney Junction has been reinstated by the Dean Forest Railway. Exhibits donated by local collectors from all these sectors are displayed at the Dean Heritage Centre.

With the decline of the iron industry before the First World War, and of the coal industry after the last, the Dean woodlands reverted to their former peacefulness. Forest Enterprise's wildlife rangers carry on the gamekeeper functions of predecessors from Saxon times. The Norman Conquest is embodied in the castle of St Briavels, the growth of monasticism in Flaxley Abbey. Of the great estates of the emerging gentry from Tudor times those at Highmeadow, the Wilderness and Clearwell Castle have been broken up but survive at Flaxley Abbey and Lydney Park. In towns and villages a handful of coaching inns represent centuries of civic and social life, as at Coleford's Angel Hotel, Ruardean's Malt Shovel and the Speech House – forest lodge and court house turned hotel in the last century. More humble hostelries continue the traditions of working class social life, home of sports and games clubs, and in older times of thrift clubs and trade union branches. High days and holidays were celebrated by numerous brass bands, Sundays by passionate sermons at dozens of Nonconformist chapels and established churches.

The choice of people and places visited below is inevitably selective and I am indebted to the hundreds of other Foresters – and 'foreigners' – interviewed over the past seven years for contributing to this portrait of the Forest's past and present diversity. For enabling me to write about the Dean I am grateful to the *Forest of Dean and Wye Valley Review*, its editor John Powell, general manager Colin Jones and the rest of the staff who make the publication possible. For his patience in being dragged uncomplainingly to many out-of-the-way places, I owe a lot to photographer Steve Cassidy. Thanks are also due to the Gloucestershire County Council Library Service, and in particular Heather Geddes and her staff at the Lydney branch. Above all I salute all those who keep the Forest's institutions alive and vigorous – bands and choirs, churches and chapels, parish and town councils, football, cricket and rugby teams, and many more besides.

While I have sought to check dates and facts with those featured, any errors remain, of course, my own.

Bob Smyth
Forest of Dean and Wye Valley Review
The Marina, Lydney
August 1998

CHAPTER 1

Foresters

'I took a team across to Normandy to see how the French handle their natural regeneration methods of re-growing woodland,' said the Forest's Deputy Surveyor John Everard. 'When I got back I was looking through old records and found the Deputy Surveyor of a hundred years ago had made the same trip for the same reason.' A photograph of the 1896 visit now hangs on the wall of Coleford's Bank House Forest Enterprise headquarters next to a montage of photographs of John's predecessors back to Edward Machen. Having retired aged seventy-one in 1854, Machen is represented by a portrait.

Forestry is a craft both changing and unchanging. More than any other British forest, the Forest of Dean displays both continuity and sometimes violent evolution. Its oldest oak groves differ little in appearance from those hunted by William the Conqueror. Yet in a thousand years since then the Dean has seen a complexity of development, industrial as well as silvicultural, which has created a landscape with a unique character.

Arriving at Bank House in 1977, John Everard faced the job of managing a vast woodland area complicated by the existence within it of half a town (Cinderford) and some twenty villages. (The office is also responsible for all the Forestry Commission woodlands in Gloucestershire, Herefordshire, Wiltshire, North Somerset and Bristol.) After beginning a forestry career as an apprentice in the Forestry Commission's extensive Monmouthshire woodlands on the west of the Wye, John was sent to their Forest Training School at Parkend's former ironworks engine house. Having been based in Bank House in 1904 shortly after being established, it moved to Parkend. It continues at Coalway's forest fringe as a place for top-up courses for foresters from around the Forest Enterprise domain.

Dispatched to gain a forestry degree, John thereafter worked in woodlands in Scotland, Hampshire, Northumberland and Wales. At Bank House he was in charge of a fiefdom covering 11,000 hectares (27,000 acres) of which 320ha are 'waste' (the old term for open space). Having been designated the UK's first 'Forest Park' in 1938, the Dean is a tourist as well as an industrial and timber-producing area. 'Despite attracting a million and a half visitors a year, it remains a working forest,' John points out. 'Timber brings in eighty per cent of our revenue and although we currently [1992] make a loss, the aim is to at least break even and eventually make a profit.'

The loss is incurred through managing the woodlands with the intermingled aims of creating an attractive and wildlife-friendly landscape, encouraging leisure and educational use, while at the same time nurturing commercially saleable

Former Deputy Surveyor John Everard in front of Coleford's Bank House.

timber. 'For fifty years after the First World War the emphasis was on planting and harvesting fast-growing conifers which produced three times the return of slower-growing deciduous trees. From 1971 the aim was to provide a roughly fifty-fifty mix, so everyone is more or less happy.'

Tourism was also encouraged to such an extent that, as he remarks, 'On a fine summer's day the Forest is technically full up – in the sense that every car park space is occupied. But even on peak days the visitor feels that he or she is in a real forest, without the pressure of other visitors you encounter in the usual country park.' For initiating what professionals call 'multipurpose forestry' he attributes credit to his predecessor Reginald ('Sandy') Sanzen-Baker, Deputy Surveyor from 1954 to 1968.

'He organized the construction of tourist facilities such as the log cabin at Symond's Yat which nowadays attracts hundreds of thousands of visitors each year. He had to hide the cost in all sorts of ways, which got him into a bit of trouble with his bosses, but he was a real pioneer – ahead of his time.' The work continued with the landscaping of redundant mining sites as picnic areas and the creation of nature reserves, including extensive lakes from former ironworks' mill ponds. In 1992 John was able to provide a central tourism visitor point with the opening of the Beechenhurst centre next to the Cannop crossroads, complete with an adjacent sculpture trail.

At the same time he was seeking to meet commercial targets set by the government. From the Domesday Book onwards the Crown sought maximum

Former Deputy Surveyors, notably (top left) Edward Machen (1808–54) and Sir James Campbell (1854–93).

financial gain from the Dean – usually with contradictory objectives provoking dissent from locals and headaches for the chief forester of the time. From bailiwicks in Norman times through the six 'walks' introduced in post-Civil War reorganization, the Forest is today run on the basis of three 'beats' maintained by teams supervised by the Bank House office. All the 'harvesting' is today done by outside contractors, timber being sold 'standing' – successful bidders cutting down the trees themselves.

An older forester George Aston (ninety) recalls the pre-war period. Born in 1918 at Sutton Lodge on the Littledean to Soudley lane, his father was forester in charge of 2,000 acres around Abbotswood and Blaize Bailey. George and his two brothers and two sisters grew up in a cottage (still standing) where drinking water came from a spring half a mile away. There was an outdoor privy and the back garden was an important source of food. 'We were better provided for in terms of food than most. We had the pig in the back, and because of the land around it a couple of milking cows as well. But we never knew the luxury of underpants until we starting earning.'

His father's job was supposed to include the pursuit of poachers. 'He turned a blind eye to that sort of thing. He took the view that they were keeping down

Woodman and preacher George Aston in front of his family's cottage, now the Cinderford cemetery gate lodge.

pests such as rabbits and deserved something for the pot.' One of George's young friends was among a group of unruly youngsters who used to shout insults at the local bobby while hidden in the bracken. 'When the policeman complained to the lad's father he was given a good hiding. Some weeks later the boy saw a light in the wood at night and went out to investigate. He saw the copper trying to snare a pheasant roosting on a bough, dazzled by his torch. After that there weren't any more complaints.'

George's father died when his son was eleven (probably as a result of being hit on the head by a cricket ball at the Foresters' annual fête at the Forest's former headquarters at Whitemead Park) and the family moved to Yew Tree Brake Lodge – now gatehouse of the Cinderford cemetery. Leaving school at fourteen, George joined a woodmen's gang. At lunchtimes he could not initially understand how the older men, enjoying a card game at the end of their 'snap', always managed to resume work before a snooping foreman appeared on the scene. 'I then realized they were keeping an ear open for the birds, who sounded an alarm signal when there was an intruder. Sometimes it was a jay, sometimes a magpie, and occasionally a carrion crow would join in, but you could always rely on a warning.'

He later worked at the Forestry Commission part-owned Parkend sawmill, which installed a bandsaw for cutting coffin boards in the late 1930s. 'Mr Chamberlain had come back from Munich waving his bit of paper and promising "Peace in our time" but our orders for coffin boards from the cities told us a different story.' During wartime fire nightwatches in hilltop towers he saw the flames from Bristol as it burned in the Blitz.

At Yew Tree Brake Lodge George welcomed Americans guarding the nearby munitions dump to Sunday services. 'The whites came in the front door, the blacks through the back so they wouldn't transgress the segregation rules. One day a regular attender was missing. A soldier friend explained he had fallen victim to mustard gas and had been buried with some others who had gone the same way in a patch of ground they named "The Graveyard" down in the plantation.'

George's father, while of no particular denomination, was a popular preacher at chapels and cottage meetings. Following in his footsteps George gave his first address aged sixteen. Thereafter he regularly preached in Wesleyan, Primitive Methodist, Bible Christian, Congregational, Brethren and Free Mission halls. He and friends also occupied the Hallelujah Tump above Cinderford's Triangle to preach the gospel each Sunday evening. 'There was a bit of catcalling from some but we were generally well received. Then in the mid- to late 1930s attendance at places of worship generally in the Dean seemed to decline.'

He became a full-time evangelist after the war, first preaching in Exmouth. 'I was then invited to Kent to help with the hop pickers mission. It snowballed from there, so we were covering half a dozen farms – or hop gardens as they call them in Kent. Then in 1967 I was invited to take on a free church in Tunbridge Wells where I stayed until a few years ago. My wife died and I had a stroke and my doctor said I ought to be in sheltered accommodation. Because my family were up here I wrote to the district council and, marvellously, they put me here.'

'Here' is the Prospect Old People's enclave down Cinderford's Victoria Road where, in his bungalow, George typed out his *Forest People* memoir and arranged for its printing. His sister and her husband who were living at Mitcheldean welcomed George for Christmas some years ago, a visit attended by his late brother. 'Myself and older brother, who remained a woodman all his life, got to reminiscing about the old days. It was the children who said I ought to write it down or it would all be forgotten.' His older sister and brother rest in the cemetery next to their old family home. His younger brother didn't return from a bombing raid over Germany.

❖ ❖ ❖

Retiring in 1997, John Everard continues to advise Forest Enterprise on the state of its woodlands and on the best felling time and price of its timber. His successor, Brian Mahony, seemed young for the post at the age of forty, until one

Former Deputy Surveyor Brian Mahony at his favourite Forest beauty spot, Mallard's Pike.

remembered that Edward Machen was only in his twenties when occupying Whitemead Park in 1808. Machen, on the other hand, had the advantage of having the job passed on from his father, who in turn was a descendant of an earlier eighteenth-century deputy surveyor. (The lineage is complicated by the two later Machens having changed their name from Davies on inheriting Machen property in English Bicknor.)

'I first discovered an enthusiasm for woods on my London school's camping trips to the New Forest,' Brian explains. 'When I asked my careers master how I went about becoming a forester, his response was, "We don't know anything about that, you will have to sort it out yourself".' So, having gained a place and subsequent forestry degree at Bangor ('where I was fortunate that the emphasis was as much on the social sciences such as geography and economics as on scientific silviculture'), in 1978 Brian was taken onto a Forestry Commission training course. 'The first day they sent me to the Forest of Dean. I had just passed my driving test and they gave me an awful old van which always had trouble starting.'

After stints in Scotland, the Lake District and North Yorkshire Moors, Brian returned to the Lake District as district manager. 'I was heavily involved in recreational use and conservation issues, liaising with agencies such as the National Park and English Nature and voluntary bodies such as the Royal Society for the Protection of Birds. The Forest of Dean was a logical progression, the Forest being bigger all round – both in acreage and in the range of woodland it covers. The only comparable area is the New Forest, which is much more open. There is a close association between the two and we work together on various issues.' In summer 1998, Brian was promoted to Operations Manager, England, based at Bristol and was succeeded by Rob Guest from York.

His employees on the ground include wildlife rangers for each of the three Forest beats, such as Eric Pritchard who works in the east. 'I was born in Moseley Green, where the family still has a cottage. My father and grandfather were both miners. Grancher went down the Fancy pit from the age of fourteen to seventy. It was one of the longest working pits, going for 140 years.' (The New Fancy, formerly owned together with the Parkend pit by Edward Protheroe, was acquired in 1883 by T.H. Deakin and others; the Deakins living in Parkend House. His son Carl inherited in 1935 and when the mine was nationalized in 1946 he became a clergyman. His son in turn became Bishop of Tewkesbury.)

Starting with the Forestry Commission as a woodman, Eric recalls a brief period of the really good old days. 'Chain-saws came in during the 1960s so as we were paid by piecework, for a time we were making good money. Then they changed the job specifications, worse luck for us.' When the wildlife rangers' jobs were created in the 1970s, he took on responsibility for managing the wildlife of his patch. 'The title may be new but the job itself is as old as the warreners who used to control the rabbits. The aim is to keep the wildlife in balance, so it doesn't get out of hand. The principle is keeping damage to the young trees to an acceptable level.'

The main threats are from squirrels, rabbits and deer. The grey squirrels are poisoned, the rabbits gassed and the deer culled by rifle. The three-hundred-strong herd of fallow deer has swelled due to animals escaping from parks elsewhere. 'You sometimes get a red deer visiting, twice the size of the fallow. There is also the occasional roe, but they move on when they find no mate.' The fallow live most of the year in small families – the doe, a yearling and a fawn – watched over by the buck, ready to see off intruding younger males. Culling takes place in winter when, as Eric explains, 'you look out for the oldest and weakest, so the breeding stock is kept healthy'.

The diversity of wildlife has increased, he says, since mixed management was introduced. 'There are a lot more raptors, for instance, than when I started. Buzzards, peregrines and sparrowhawks are much more plentiful, and there are also now the gosses – goshawks. We note where they are breeding so they are left undisturbed when there is any forestry work going on.'

Wildlife rangers Eric Pritchard (front), Neil Sollis (left) and Aubrey Neale.

Warden since 1987 of the RSPB's Nagshead nature reserve outside Parkend, Ivan Proctor (fifty-two), is also responsible for the society's conservation activities in the rest of the Forest and Lower Wye Valley – including the annual watch over the nesting peregrine falcons at Symond's Yat. He explains the curious origin of the Nagshead reserve. 'The Forestry Commission found its trees were being defoliated by caterpillars, so in 1942 they installed nest boxes to encourage more insect-eating birds. The scheme was taken over by the RSPB in 1974 and in 1985 the reserve's 350 acres were extended to take in the Commission's former nursery where thousands of seedlings were raised. The policy having changed after 1970, the nursery closed. The fields reverted to meadow, thus adding another habitat to the old oaks of the enclosure – designated an SSSI, Site of Special Scientific Interest.'

On this summer's day the birds were quiet all around us. Peak visiting time for birdwatchers is May and early June when birders flock to see the pied flycatchers that have flown in from winter quarters in tropical Africa's savannah belt. Other favourites are the redstart, which favours old oak woods, and the wood warbler. There are also butterflies – up to thirty of the forty-five or so species usually visible in Britain. Those sunning themselves on a bank of brambles, Ivan says, are

Ivan Proctor, RSPB conservation officer for the Forest and Wye Valley, at the Nagshead nature reserve.

mostly ringlets and meadow browns. Adders thrive in the grassland, basking on open patches in sunny spring weather. Dragonflies too are milling around near the ponds excavated in 1988 to increase habitat diversity. All this attracts some 500 visitors a day at summer weekends, as well as regular visits from school groups.

Other designated sites within the Forest include the Cannop Valley Forest Nature Reserve, with its ten-mile nature trail running from Nagshead to the Mireystock crossroads, and SSSIs such as the Soudley Ponds across the road from the Dean Heritage Centre. Around forty smaller sites are leased to the Gloucestershire Wildlife Trust. Also Lady Park Wood opposite the Biblins is a National Nature Reserve, the highest category of protected area. Left untouched since clearances during the war, it has been the subject of study by one of the country's foremost woodland experts. Having retired from English Nature's East Anglian headquarters, Dr George Peterken settled at St Briavels Common to be closer to Lady Park and the area's other woodlands – including a coppice within his own grounds.

So what does Ivan do in winter? 'There are plenty of sites to visit. There is the recording of the year's bird populations to work out. There are talks to societies around the Forest. There is more than enough for one person, but it is a privilege to work in such a fascinating place.'

CHAPTER 2

Miners

Climbing back up the slope to the Hopewell Colliery entrance is agony. The floor has been concreted and handrails installed in the side walls but you arrive at the surface gasping. For the first time, members of the general public can experience for themselves what working in the small old pits was like, the mine having been opened to visitors in 1997 by its owner Robin Morgan. The last but one full-time freeminer, Robin and his son Neil work the Phoenix Colliery on the other side of the road, delivering winter coal to householders around the Forest.

Hopewell was a busy mine even since the war, up to nineteen men working there before its closure in 1985. It opened in 1821, being part-owned from 1841 by the Revd Howard Hinton of London and known as 'Hinton's' to the end of its working life. Fixing you up with miner's lamp and heavy battery strapped around the waist, Robin leads the way underground. 'Pause a bit and let your eyes get accustomed to the dark,' he advises. 'I've put in handrails for safety's sake but I didn't put in lighting because I wanted visitors to see for themselves how it felt to be dependent on the lamps.'

The 'road' descends steeply to the working level. A side gallery reveals a seam of coal glistening in the beam of light. 'Lovely stuff, that is,' says Robin picking up a loose chunk. 'They hacked it out lying on their sides. Today at the Phoenix we have a cutter which does twelve feet at a time, a chute tipping it into six wagons.' He points to a groove in the roof, where the colliers chiselled holes in the rock – sixteen around the sides of the advancing tunnel. 'Then they put in black powder and blew the section down.'

Pointing to the pit props he has newly installed, Robin explains that it isn't a matter of the roof descending but of the floor rising once the pressure is removed. As we reach the original workings, entered from the Wimberry side of the hill, he indicates the fine unmortared stonework still forming an immaculate horseshoe arch. Gesturing towards a cavity in the tunnel side, he says, 'They dug an opening up to the surface and when a fire was lit it drew in fresh air from the entrance. As the road progressed they blocked this one up and dug another further in.'

We arrive at the lower entrance with its blissful sunlight and trees beyond the gate through which visitors leave to return to the minehead up a gentle track. 'I seem to have forgotten the key,' Robin mutters. Desperately rattling the bars, I am whimpering with frustration. As we begin the painful walk back up, Robin says cheerfully, 'During the three years it's taken to get it in shape I have been in and out at least twenty times a day.' For himself and the colliers carrying tools after a strenuous shift, it must have taken almost superhuman resilience. In Robin's case

Freeminer Robin Morgan in his Hopewell Colliery, the first to be opened to visitors.

the hardihood was already proven. Before acquiring the Phoenix and Hopewell mines he worked as a kerb-layer, the *Guinness Book of Records* citing him as fastest kerbstone-layer in the world.

❖ ❖ ❖

Responsible for regulating Forest mines since before 1692 has been the Deputy Gaveller, in charge of awarding the 'gales' – the areas where mines could be dug. Born in Coalway, the son of a miner, Albert Howell (seventy-five) first worked as an accountant for the Forest of Dean collieries (joint) selling scheme. Following wartime service in the RAF flying nightfighters, he returned to a job transformed by the 1946 nationalization of the largest pits. After looking after the smaller mines he moved in 1950 to Bank House and the Deputy Gaveller's office (the post of Gaveller being vested in the Forestry Commission, formerly the Crown).

'We had seven people working in the office in those days. Our job was to check output, collect royalties and check for misdemeanours such as trespassing on other gales. We also had what you would today call a health and safety role. If you saw something going wrong you pointed it out.' He pulls out the ledger from that year, one of the many old registers stacked around the room. The record of royalties paid per ton showed six big NCB pits operating: Eastern United (1909–59), Northern United (1934–65), Norchard, Princess Royal (1842–1962), Cannop (1907–60) and Lydbrook's Arthur and Edward, or Waterloo (1830s–1959). Thirty-six small mines were functioning, the total output for the

Forest that year being 724,000 tons. 'That was the heyday. Now the most easily accessible reserves are exhausted. Only the highly inclined seams are left.'

Of the small miners' life he says, 'They used to have an average of three people working at each: a dad with his son or neighbour and the lady of the house on the engine outside! It's a hell of a game. The digging is hard enough but then when you've sold off the small stuff to the Coal Board you have to go round selling the domestic stuff.' Apart from the two full-time freeminers, his records showed fifty paying rents ranging from £5 a year to £60 depending on how long ago the gale was taken out. 'A lot are kept on by aged people who hope they will get bought out. One prospective opencast operator holds twenty gales at Lightmoor. Then there are those who aren't licensed to extract but hold a gale to prevent others working it – usually near housing – so the county council has three and the district council two.'

Deputy Gaveller from 1973 to 1997, Albert's workload had declined after the closing of the last deep pit in 1965. Carrying on with the job into his retirement years, he explained that in the 1980s it mostly involved providing statements for prospective house builders about conditions underground. For this purpose dozens of maps of long-gone mines were stored in rolls in racks around the walls, a two-pronged fork propped nearby to lift off the highest. 'You have to couch the report in terms of "ifs" and "probablys" because you can never be sure settlement isn't going to happen.' He begins to explain the complex procedure for allocating a gale that becomes vacant, but then shrugs. 'It's now academic. The mines are only of interest to a few freeminers and geology students.'

There have been 4,339 names registered as freeminers since 1838, qualification being dependent on being born within the Hundred of St Briavels and by working a year and a day in a Forest mine. (It used to be thought that it was a year and a day 'underground' but Redbrook's Mike Jones won a court case which ruled he qualified from having worked in opencasting. There are also 317 free quarry men.) The exact number of those extant is unknown, even to officers of the Freeminers' Association.

Their secretary is Ray Wright (sixty-eight), owner of Clearwell Caves, the complex of iron mines he opened to the public in 1968 and now runs with his freeminer son, Jonathan. 'My father's mother came from the area and after the

Former Deputy Gaveller Albert Howell with maps of long-dead mines.

Ray Wright at his Clearwell Caves former iron mine, where he still extracts iron oxides and ochre for paint pigments.

1914–18 war he used to visit here on a motorbike researching the family history. He married a girl from the Cridlands family and they moved back here in 1937 when I was seven. We lived in a cottage at Gunn's Mill at Flaxley. My father was handy as a carpenter, cabinet maker and pattern maker, so he was useful at the mill. Among other things he used to repair the wooden buckets of the mill wheel which drove the circular saw for cutting logs. It was also used for chopping up straw and hay to make chaff as animal feed.'

Ray earned pocket money helping the farmer, Mr Fred Ryder, with cider making, cutting hay and other tasks around the farm. In leisure time he explored the caves round about. Leaving school at thirteen, he worked at the Grange Court railway depot checking in loads to the Christy and Vesey yard. Later he worked at Rank Xerox as leader of a section designing new photocopiers. Buying the Clearwell mine, he spent weekends and holidays for the next ten years doing the place up. 'The only brick building here was a pigscot [sty]. The stone engine house was just a pile of rubble.'

Only two galleries were at first visitable. Today there are nine, with deeper caverns – reaching six hundred feet below ground – accessible to groups by arrangement. Ray and Jonathan continue mining; not for ore but for the iron oxides, especially ochre, of various colours which, when ground up, are the basis for paints and cosmetics. As well as assisting at Clearwell, Jonathan supervises work at their other mine – the Lea Bailey level north of Drybrook. This was the site of a famous scam a century or so ago, its promoters claiming it was a goldmine. There are traces of gold but Ray's interest is in possibly opening it as another mining museum in the future.

Four years ago Ray was elected one of the Forest's four Verderers, the officials charged with supervising the 'vert and the venison' – the trees and the deer. 'We meet every forty days or so at the Verderer's Court in the Speech House where the Forest officers – Deputy Surveyor and Land Agent – inform us how the deer herds are being managed and how the timber is being looked after. They tell us how visitor amenities are progressing and in 1997 we have been considering the minerals plan put out by the county council. The Forestry Commission has been drawing up its own plan and we will be looking at this as well.'

❖ ❖ ❖

The Deputy Gaveller is technically responsible for stone quarries as well as mines. 'My colleague across the corridor is the area land agent for the Forestry Commission: he looks from the grass roots up and I look from the grass roots down,' explains the Deputy Gaveller since 1997, John Harvey (fifty-seven). Born in Wales he went underground straight after leaving school. 'There were fifty-two pits in South Wales when I started, so at the time mining seemed to offer a good career. By the 1970s the writing was on the wall, so I switched to the factory inspectorate.

'I was based in Gloucester, which was a bonus because I had many links with the Forest. My grandmother and grandfather lived at Beulah Cottage on the Kymin, a great aunt nearby, and another in Monmouth – so I remember childhood visits to the area in the 1940s. My grandmother moved to Hillside Cottage in Coleford. She was listed in the *Guinness Book of Records* as the world's oldest living person at the time, being 114 when she died.'

In 1979 he and two partners worked the New Found Out mine at Edge End. 'I don't think I've ever been so fit in my life. We were using the old methods, of course, with timber supports and the rest, which was a bit ironic since I had been trained in all the most modern techniques. But the price of coal was then quite high – £50 to £60 a ton for house coal and maybe £32 a ton for small coals for power stations. Now that last figure is down to £25.' After three years the mine was worked out and John started a small building business. He carried on with mine and cave consultancy work and was

Deputy Gaveller John Harvey at his former New Found Out mine, Edge End.

part-time assistant to the Deputy Gaveller who had succeeded Albert Howell on his final retirement, fellow Welshman Roy Piggott (seventy).

Having been apprenticed as a mine engineer in his native South Wales during the war, Roy became the NCB's regional chief surveyor for the South Western region, covering 94 collieries and 1,598 licensed mines in South Wales, Monmouthshire, the Dean and Somerset. From the 1960s he was an international consultant, retiring in 1994 to continue as a freelance – including the part-time job of Deputy Gaveller. 'I was conned,' he chuckles heartily. 'It was to be only collecting the rent for four small mines. I saw myself sitting with feet up on the table, cup of coffee in hand, doing the newspaper crossword.

'Instead, it's Armageddon. There's MPs, journalists and television crews everywhere. It's all gone mad, I tell you. I should have known there were problems in the Forest of Dean but no one said anything about what a can of worms it would be. There is no subsidence, they told me. Well there has been since I arrived. It's my own fault, I suppose. I've a jinx. Then there is Severn Trent Water pumping water without permission into a shaft of the old Northern United colliery, which is making the adjacent shaft unstable. The water table has already risen a metre.'

Roy launches into a fluent recapitulation of relevant legislation since the 1838 Forest Mines Act, the ramifications of the 1994 Act creating the Coal Authority, and the dispute about whether freeminers needed to be licensed by the Authority – and how much royalty it might be allowed to charge. He adds that when the NCB closed down the Forest mines he suggested keeping a couple of pit heads standing because of their educational value, 'but they ignored the idea'. It was also Roy who, in his earlier job in the 1960s, designed the pipe from the Norchard mine which, at the lowest point of the Dean basin, could drain water into the River Lyd.

'When the last mine closed in 1965 the pumping stopped,' John Harvey continues the story. 'The mines began filling with water but because the deep mines were below sea level it took years for the shafts to fill up to ground level. Then one day this excitable Welshman, Roy, came on the phone to say water was coming out of the pipe. "It's working, it's working," he shouted.' Today the pipe can be seen at the Norchard Steam Centre entrance through which twenty-five million litres a day drains into the stream, an awesome reminder of the problem which plagued the coalfield throughout its life and eventually brought about its death.

John was involved from the start in public meetings, consultations with government officials and legal advisors, and press conferences at locations such as Hayners Bailey, the mine run by the other full-time freeminer, Gerald Haynes. 'Today there are nine mines either working, or exploratory, or tourist – plus the Clearwell Caves which represent several iron mine gales. Some are hobby mines, where people are getting work experience to register as freeminers or to keep the tradition going.'

While the freeminers will eventually disappear because of the lack of a maternity ward within the Hundred of St Briavels since that at the Dilke Hospital closed, individual ownership of existing mines could continue for ever. 'Once a gale has been registered by a freeminer he can pass it on or sell it to anyone else.

And even if every mine closed tomorrow there would be problems from the collapse of old workings stretching for the foreseeable future. I am not saying there are a lot of disasters waiting to happen but you have to keep an eye on things. When you have had people digging under-ground for two thousand years, subsi-dence is going to be here forever.

'The iron mines pose more of a problem than the coal mines. At Crossways a trans-former station on a farm disappeared into the old Coleford iron mines. There have been several collapses of shafts at Bream, so the Coal Authority spends money each year on capping or recapping shafts – especially in places visited by tourists. Then there was the dumping of waste down old shafts which may have long-term consequences. The 1995 Environmental Act refers to controlled waters which have to be monitored.'

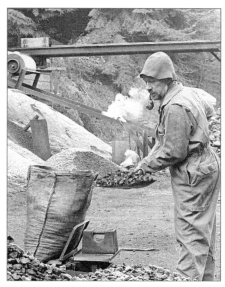

Freeminer Gerald Haynes at his Hayners Bailey mine at Cannop.

One of the few advantages of the Dean coalfield was that it didn't have the firedamp gasses that elsewhere could suffocate or kill miners by explosions. There was always the danger of foul air if ventilation was inadequate but miners could work with naked lamps in pre-electricity days. The water on the other hand not only required expensive pumping but posed a constant threat of flooding from adjacent old unpumped shafts. Ernest Davies (eighty-nine) was one of those involved in the near-disaster at Waterloo in 1949.

'My father, grandfather and great grandfather were all in the pits,' he says at his Cinderford home, one of the first to be built in the Denecroft estate. 'Just before the First World War the family moved to South Wales to seek work. So although I went to Ruardean Woodside's Slad school, I started work in one of the pits there, earning five shillings a week, which was good money in those days.'

Moving back to Steam Mills he went to work at Lydbrook's Waterloo colliery, also known as the Arthur and Edward. 'It was all Crawshays then. They were good employers, or at least I found them so. If anything was wanting to be done around the pit it was me they asked to do it. The first we knew of something wrong was when the men came up from the road beneath us. They sure were travelling! They said, "Come on, we've got to get out, the water has broken in."

'I followed my mates off the face. When I got into the road I put my tools on the bar and the others did the same. I found myself leading my mates out. When I got to the heading leading to the new pit I went to see what the water was like. It sure was coming out with a force, hitting the back wall and going towards the pit

Freeminers Association past treasurer Harold Powell (in cap) confronts Coal Authority chief executive Neville Washington (in hard hat) at a meeting arranged by Paul Marland (centre), the Forest's MP, 1979–97.

bottom. I went back up to where my mates were waiting, took them through a road leading to the return, and went down to the main road leading to the pit bottom.

'The water was at least two feet high. Tallow – I think his surname was Lewis – said how many pumps there were at the pit bottom. I said I couldn't care how many there were, they couldn't cope. Just after that Ron Carter came down the way we did and said, "I've got to go and get the two men who were driving a road down to meet up with the 80 dipper to shorten the air route." He had to go against the flood, which took some doing the rate the water was travelling. When he came back he said he had just been on the phone to the pit bottom and Mr Marfell had said we had to go on out.

'We started out and at first it was not too bad but when the water started to hit your stomach it was that cold that at every step it took your breath away. We got almost to where we got in on the journey to work, but there was a dip in the road and it looked as though the water was up to the roof. We were by where the water went to the pit bottom to be pumped out. When we reached the pit bottom we had to clamber over the full trams of coal the water was so high. We made it out with only five minutes to spare. When we got on the trams the water was up to our necks already. It was my my cousin Harry Turner who let down a drive of trams to the pit bottom. He did a good job there or we wouldn't have got out.'

Waterloo closed soon after and Ernest moved briefly to Northern United. 'The manager there thought he was God, so I didn't stop.' Instead he joined a building firm constructing the first extension at Rank Xerox, whose expansion in these years was some compensation for the disappearing collieries.

CHAPTER 3
Landscapes

At Lower Perrygrove Farm outside Coleford, Ray Prosser (sixty-eight) produces a photo of himself as an infant with his dad in the courtyard of Stowe Grange. The Grange, originally a grange of Monmouth's Grace Dieu monastery, became part of the great Clearwell Court estate, auctioned off in 1907 when Thomas Prosser was tenant of the 192-acre farm. This estate and several others were bought by the Crown Commissioners who remain landlords of dozens of Forest farms. When they sold off surplus properties in 1971 the Grange was acquired by Oxford don William Parker but the Prossers carried on farming the surrounding land.

His father died when Ray was only one. 'My brother ran the farm for a few years during the war, but I took over at the age of fourteen to help my mother. She were an excellent manager, mind.' He married his wife Sheila at a date which eludes him. 'I shall have to ask the boss,' he says, going out of the large kitchen. 'It were 1952,' he announces on his return, adding that at that time they farmed the adjacent Longley Farm. 'It were mostly dairy cows and sheep. We had about six hundred ewes to lamb each year.'

As a kid Ray helped out at the nearby Lower Perrygrove and Breckness Court farms owned by his uncle Mostyn Watkins. Part of the former was occupied by Puzzle Wood, the Victorian name for the weirdly overgrown scowles covering several acres. 'I used to love visiting Puzzle Wood. I used to sweep the paths at four or five years of age and generally keep things tidy.' When his uncle died in 1980, Ray bought it at the ensuing auction and moved in.

Today, after a heart attack some years ago, he has a few cows, pigs and sheep, as well as Shetland ponies and Highland cattle, and is helped by younger son Geoff. Like other farmers in the area he is a regular attender at Gloucester's Monday market and bitter critic of the CAP (Common Agricultural Policy) system. 'You have got to buy your milk quotas and suchlike things nowadays. It's blinking terrible.' In his own form of agricultural diversification, Ray's main business nowadays is running the Wood for visitors.

'It was owned in the late 1800s by the Turners from Cardiff who had the woodland landscaped with seats and bridges for their own enjoyment. They christened it Puzzle Wood because it's such a maze to get around.' It is indeed, with some paths following the bottom of 'churns' excavated by Roman miners, others climbing the mini-cliffs above. The limestone is covered with thick mosses. Luxuriant ferns sprout from crevices. Trees push up from the bare rock with their tangled roots exposed. In spring there is wild garlic and a profusion of bluebells.

Ray Prosser in the Puzzle Wood woodland of his Lower Perrygrove farm.

'The seasons are all over the place these days but the bluebells are usually out in late April.' It is a good time to visit because of the birdsong, he suggests, though it can enjoyably be visited in the unrolling seasons. As the leaves emerge, climax and turn golden, the wood takes on different characteristics.

'Uncle Mostyn bought it around the turn of the century and kept it in its original state. It had a few visitors but nothing commercial.' Ray improved access and visitor facilities, with Professor Parker's wife selling tickets at the entrance which provide the income for its upkeep. While he has put it on the market, Ray admits he is reluctant to sell in case it is over-commercialized. He mentions the visit ten years or so ago when two Turner sisters arrived with their mother for her eighty-nineth birthday outing. 'We gave them tea and the old lady pointed to where she said there was a spiral staircase in the middle of the house, now covered up. There was an' all, but of the wood itself she said nothing had altered since she had seen it last at seven years old.'

❖ ❖ ❖

Ron Aldridge (eighty-four) was born at Whitecroft mill where his father was miller, as well as being manager of The Lydney District Farmers' Ltd – the agricultural supplies cooperative launched by the first Lord Bledisloe in 1904. At sixteen Ron was put to work in the depot. 'My first job was standing at the bottom of the chute holding bags to be filled with animal feed. We never put meat in the animal feed – ever, ever, ever. Our mixes were confidential but if a farmer wanted to come into the office he would be shown the formula. Then I was put in the office and after that I was sent out as a salesman visiting local farms.'

Monday was Gloucester market, which Ron still visits most weeks to keep in touch. Tuesday was the Rodley round. Farmers sat waiting for him, smoking old pipes and offering him a glass of home-brewed cider. Ron being a well-known Methodist, they knew he would refuse but it was a good excuse for a glass themselves. As Ron recounts in his *The Country Corn Merchant*, reminiscences he published himself, most farmers in the 1930s were barely making a living. Wednesday was an opportunity to supplement their income at the Grange Court station fruit and egg market. Plums were auctioned off and eggs taken to Cheltenham for grading. With a few shillings in their pocket, the smallholders adjourned to the Junction Inn for a natter.

Former corn merchant and noted sportsman Ron Aldridge at his paddock above Lydney.

Thursday was the Littledean area. Friday began at Mitcheldean, with Gloucester market again on Saturday morning. A noted sportsman, Ron spent weekends playing various games. He played hockey for Gloucestershire and the West of England, played badminton at county level, and for many years captained the Lydney Cricket Club (also founded by Lord Bledisloe). Having become the Farmers' stores manager on his father's retirement, he was secretary of the National Farmers' Union Lydney branch, Rotary member and secretary of the Forest's Methodist youth association.

The second week of the cycle began once again at Gloucester market, accompanied by calls in the Minsterworth area. Tuesday saw him in Elton and Popes Hill, where Olly Broughton would comment on his weekend cricketing performance: 'Bisn't much good with the bat, bist?' Flaxley Abbey being on his rounds, he ate lunchtime sandwiches in the head gardener's potting shed (in front of a welcome fire in winter). Wednesday's Grange Court market was followed by the Thursday round starting at Blaisdon. At Boseley Farm was Bert Phelps, whose son Humphrey took on Boseley Court Farm.

The co-op ceased trading a few years ago, long after his own retirement, but Ron's brother Geoff continues in the Whitecroft mill. A familiar village character, he was once 'mayor', presiding over a mock court at the Crown Inn. Geoff is also president of Lydney's Royal British Legion, his wife Jean plays piano at the Miner's Arms, and their son looks after the cattle on Turnout Farm. In front of his own house above Lydney was a field allowing an extensive view over the

Severn. It looks prime building land. Ron nodded, 'But I've bought it, so no one can build on it in my time.'

Vestiges of once extensive apple orchards can be seen all over the Forest plateau's slopes, formerly providing the rough cider which is still the favoured drink of older Foresters. So valued was it that gales were not allowed to be dug under buildings, back gardens, churchyards or orchards. Land on the east of the plateau was especially favourable for plums, those of Blaisdon becoming famous. 'It is a unique micro-climate here,' explains Captain Bill Swinley RN, whose family was based at Flaxley Abbey and has held farms hereabouts for centuries. 'The tide coming up the Severn pushes warm air in front of it which spreads around the lower part of the valley, so the fruit trees never suffer from frost in the flowering season. It hits the hills of the Forest of Dean and doesn't go much further up the estuary.'

After an active service life, Bill Swinley, now in his sixties, came to be custodian of what the Countryside Commission describes as 'probably the most interesting old orchards in the West of England'. He lives at Broughtons, a wisteria-festooned house on a slight rise above the Flaxley road, built by the family two hundred years ago. At the peak of his career, having commanded submarines and frigates, Bill was seconded to create and then command the Bahamas Defence Force as Commodore of their sizeable fleet of patrol boats trying to control drug smuggling between South America and the USA. A 1980s press photo shows Bill's boat back in port, off-loading hundreds of kilos of captured cannabis. As he shows us around the orchards he walks with the aid of a finger stick. 'They bashed me around a bit when we caught up with them,' he mentions. 'But we bashed them up a bit more!'

On annual leave he and wife Jenny returned for holidays, staying in a caravan on Haylings Farm, below Popes Hill, in the centre of seventeen acres of old apple, pear and plum trees. 'The orchards were of no commercial value so we opened up on a pick-your-own basis more than twenty years ago. Our customers came from miles around and kept coming back each year. Among them are Hungarians and Czechs who have settled in Wales, wanting the fruit to make plum wines and brandies.'

The orchards include some twenty species of plum and many species each of apple and pear. They are nowadays looked after by Countryside Commission specialists in a conservation project recommended by the Ministry of Agriculture and the county's Farming and Wildlife Advisory Group, who have also been planting new trees. For the trees are interesting not only for their fruit but for the birdlife they support. Their trunks are so aged and gnarled their bark is an insect paradise. Birds come to feed and nest, woodpeckers taking up residence in dead trees left standing. Apples and pears are harvested by residents of the local Camphill Village Trust, as is the mistletoe each Christmas which grows in profusion on the unsprayed trees.

Bill has also added, more or less by accident, a different kind of habitat in a neighbouring field. 'There was a cattle pond there, so we thought we might provide a commercial fishing lake. It dried up in the great drought of 1976, so we dug down and found a spring. After that we excavated the lake as you see it, leaving an island in the middle. The fish we put in became so used to being fed each day the idea of game fishing went out of the window. There is one old trout in particular who puts on a display which involves snatching pieces of bread in an upward leap. When spectators applaud, it does it a second time. It's a very dangerous place: I can spend hours here just watching the wildlife.'

Bill was featured a couple of years ago in BBC Radio 4's Sunday morning *On Your Farm* programme in which he repeated his conservationist message. 'Twenty per cent of Britain's young orchards were grubbed up this year because they weren't making a profit. Fifty per cent of plums on sale in the shops come from abroad. It is very sad

Captain Bill Swinley RN among his historic orchards below Popes Hill.

that although we produce the best plums in the world we are importing inferior products. I arranged a tasting last year. Of a row of bowls of plums which visitors could sample, they said the last one tasted like cotton wool. "That's the foreign one I bought from the greengrocer's to see if there's a difference," I told them.'

The programme produced a curious response. While he was cooking breakfast for the interviewer, he let the pancakes burn – and admitted that since his wife died he had found it difficult to cope with the housekeeping. The phone started ringing and letters arriving from ladies offering their services as housekeeper – and even matrimony. He wasn't tempted but two years ago met the widow of a Buckinghamshire arable farmer and they married this year.

Bill Swinley's Fruit

PLUMS

Bella de Louvain	Marjorie Seeding
Black Diamond	Monarch
Blaisdon	Opal
Bullace	Ouillins Golden Gage
Cambridge Gage	Pershore Yellow Egg
Cox's Emperors	Queen of the Gages
Czar	Rivers Early Prolific
Edwards	Sanctus Hubertus
Giant Prune	Shropshire Giant Damson
Late Prolific	Victorias (several variations)

PEARS

Blakeney Red	Diana Bisoche
Blakeney Green	Honey Nab
Brewers Hardy	Pitmarston Duchess
Bossop	Strawberry Pear
Conference	Williams
Commice	Winter Bergamie
Claps Favourite	

APPLES

Beauty of Bath	Overleaf
Bramley (Red & Green)	Tom Putt
Edwards	Russett
Keswick Codling	Underleaf
(King of Popes Hill)	Winter Blenheim
Lord Derby	Newton Wonder

NEW ADDITIONS

Adams Permain	Gellway Pippin
Allington Pipper	Kirs of the Pippin
Annie Elizabeth	Orleans Reinette
Ashmeads Kernel	Pitmaster Pineapple
Blenheim Orange	Red Peasgood Nonsuch
Cotshead	Rosemary Russett
Cornish Gillyflower	Stirling Castle
Court Pendy Plat	White Melrose
Court of Wick	William Crump
D'Arcy Spice	Winston

On the former railway bridge between Stowfield and Welsh Bicknor on a weekday morning, workers from the adjacent SCA packaging factory (the former Cable Works) were enjoying elevenses sandwiches and a spot of sunshine. Below, two fishermen were mooring a boat at the Wye Fisheries jetty where a sign reads: 'No trespassers on boats. Survivors will be prosecuted.' Having stowed his equipment in the fisheries pavilion workshed, water bailiff George Woodward mourned that 1997 was the worst year for salmon fishing since he had arrived on the river. 'In places where you used to be able to catch eighteen salmon, this year we were down to one. If it carries on like this there will be none left at all.'

George came from Shropshire to work for the Courtfield estate, living at a cottage in Welsh Bicknor. He looked after a three-mile stretch of river, divided into six beats, three of which were hired out to syndicates who were allowed six rods plus two guests for a weekly visit. In the late 1980s boom years, clients paid £1,400 a rod per year, with only an outside chance of catching a small number of salmon. 'On beats near Monmouth where the chances are good of catching more fish a year, the cost is £2,200,' explained George's daughter Lynn back in 1992. In those days she was employed as Britain's only female ghillie, working for four years as George's assistant.

Lynn and George Woodward, water bailiffs, at Stowfield's old railway bridge.

'My dad taught me everything I know about the river, the fish and their habits. In Shropshire, as an only child, I spent all my free time roaming the countryside. I had my first fishing rod at four and a half, a cheap one from Woolworths, and used to fish for wild trout. Later it was coarse fish, eel and pike but after thirteen I lost interest.' After school she trained as a potter but was attracted to the Wye. As well as working for her father, she met Hugh – the young gamekeeper for the Bishopswood estate, a thousand acres let to a shooting syndicate. 'Those involved in estate work tend to mix together, it's a world of its own,' she explains. 'Hugh and Dad went stalking together and it grew from there.'

Lynn took clients out in an outboard-motor-powered boat. 'You take them to the best place from previous experience. The trick is to get the boat in exactly the right place for the client who sits in front. Even a few inches can make a difference. In muddy water the salmon can't see the bait unless it's very close. In summer in addition the fish tend to get very dopey. Towards autumn the cock fish get very aggressive and territorial. They tend to grab hold of anything that comes near them, not because they want to eat it but because it irritates them.'

She explained the life cycle of this king of fishes – how it spawns in the upper reaches of rivers like the Wye, but grows up in the seas around Greenland before returning to its home river to reproduce. 'Two sea winter fish, as we call them, come back weighing around 15 lb – three sea winter fish at five years old at 20 lb plus.' Their decline in recent years she explains as resulting from changes in the spawning beds above Rhyader, excessive netting around Greenland – and poaching.

Lynn was a reserve bailiff, patrolling at night with walkie-talkie equipment which kept her in touch with nine full-time bailiffs based at Monmouth. She also assisted on Bishopswood estate work. 'I go stalking with a rifle because the deer need culling and I also shoot a lot of rabbits.' Even if salmon was available she wouldn't eat it. 'I don't like it, in the same way my dad won't eat venison. Nor pheasants, which he calls "my babies", having reared them up.'

She had just lost her ghillie job. A new owner had bought the fishing rights, mainly for his own and his family's pleasure, and at a much reduced price from the yuppie '80s. While he allowed George to hire out the river to three rods for three days of the week in return for looking after the rest, it was not a sufficient livelihood for both of them. 'Perhaps I'll get my kiln fixed up and start making pots again,' she laughed philosophically. As it turned out, she moved away to work on an estate in mid-Wales.

A footnote to the old Wye ways is provided by Tim Oakes of Lydbrook who makes coracles. They were banned from the river in the 1920s in an attempt, even then, to preserve dwindling fish stocks. Only one specimen survived, which records showed was preserved somewhere in the Gloucestershire museum service – but no one knew where. With only written descriptions to work from, Tim started on his prototype. 'It was rather like building a Ford Anglia from an old handbook.'

With a licence from Forest Enterprise to collect wood from the Forest, he cut hazel for the boat's rim and ordered laths for its ribs. Soaking the latter in a water-filled trench in his back garden, he bent them into shape and covered them with tightly stretched canvas daubed with bitumen. When dried, the skin was so tough it broke the blade of a Stanley knife. Yet the finished product is so light the fishermen could carry it on their backs to and from the river.

Tim took his (in the back of a van) to south Wales where a few coracles survive and where there is the world's only coracle museum. It was much admired but different from the Welsh craft. In Wales the rivers are short and fast running, so their coracles are small with high gunwales. On the Severn, which is broad and flat, they were large and round. On the Wye they were a cross between the two. There were even variations at different parts of the Wye, those at Ross being bigger than elsewhere. In the last century you could hire a coracle there, spend a day fishing while floating down river, and have the boat brought back up on a horse and cart.

A musicologist by trade, Tim settled in the Forest having pleasant memories of it from a holiday here when he was seven. 'I cried when my parents took me back,' he recalls. Having built the first of what are now half a dozen or so coracles, he was relieved to find a photograph of the Wye's most famous coracle fisherman

'The man with the little boats', Lydbrook coracle-maker Tim Oakes.

– Lydbrook's own William Drew – from the last century. 'It looked almost exactly like mine, which I then called "Mr Drew".' He later found the museum's example (in the travelling collection), gives talks on the subject, and has visited Scotland and Ireland where they make larger sea-going coracles called 'curraghs'. Having also been filmed for a BBC TV children's programme, he says he is now recognized by local children in shops. 'They say, "There's the man with the small boat."'

When Frank and Margaret Baber moved into Green Cottage on Watery Lane at the edge of the Lydney Park estate the garden didn't exist. The ground was ploughed up and sown and when the mower couldn't cope with the grass they imported sheep. 'They arrived two at a time in a Reliant Robin,' Margaret recalls. 'It was quite a sight.' Frank was from a long-established farming family at Awre and Churcham, Margaret a domestic science teacher at the grammar school. They mapped out a plan for the garden, planted ornamental trees and cleared the banks of the stream to create a mysterious bog garden.

The garden, which opens during summer for the National Gardens Scheme (established in 1927 initially to support the Queen's Nursing Institute), offers the bonus of a spectacular display of peonies. 'When I started planting them in 1980 there were only two specialist suppliers left in the country. Even the RHS – Royal Horticultural Society – said it had no peony expert. So I took over the vegetable

Frank and Margaret Baber with dog Rosie at their Green Cottage garden, Lydney.

garden and began building up a range of varieties. I found some in France, and corresponding with the American Peony Society brought me others.'

Today the bed is a National Reference Collection with eighty named varieties and another twenty or so awaiting identification. Margaret has become coordinator of the Peony Group of the Hardy Plant Society and finds herself in touch with enthusiasts from Scandinavia to New Zealand. 'One of the joys of gardening is that people want to share their knowledge. I keep a list of what visitors have asked for and when I've got a surplus I get in touch.'

The hybrid peonies flower in May, the rest in June, but the garden opens as early as March for the brookside hellebores. 'We couldn't cope without the help of neighbours,' Margaret explains. 'They look after the gate and teas while I handle the plant stall.' A visit to Green Cottage also provides the opportunity for a glance at the remains of the dam which once formed the Black Pond feeding one of the Lydney iron forges – among the town's few surviving industrial monuments.

Millend House overlooks the Whitecliff Brook running down to Newland, the Tremletts having come here thirty years ago when John was manager of the Whitecliff quarry. He is humping stone chippings towards a Japanese garden he is creating following a trip to Japan, but claims that 'it is my wife who is the real gardener'. April leads off on a tour of the hillside, which was more or less wilderness when they arrived. 'The rooks haven't nested this year,' she remarks in the woodland with its Scots pines planted in Victorian times. 'They say they can tell if the trees are no longer healthy, although it might be a matter of buzzards taking chicks from the nests.'

She talks with a shudder of the storm of 1990 which brought down many of the trees. 'It was the year we were first going to open to the public and it was a panic sorting it all out before they arrived.' We return by the rose garden and other formal beds, in the middle of which is a neat vegetable garden with ornamental pond and sitting-out area. As well as opening the garden under the 'gardens for charity' scheme, with proceeds going to the local branch of the Macmillan Nurses – whose volunteers assist with the teas – April runs the house as a B&B guest

April Tremlett at her Millend House garden, Newland.

house for those with a special interest in gardens. She is also well known as a flower arranger, giving demonstrations for NAFAS – the National Association of Flower Arranging Societies – for more than twenty years. 'There are clubs dotted around all over the place – Lydney, Monmouth, Ross and Whitchurch, for example – but I've given talks as far afield as Germany.

'It was in my childhood in Northern Ireland that I developed an interest in flowers. In those days you could go for a walk and pick what you wanted and botanize. Some flowers have disappeared since then but others are coming back. There were a lot of cowslips once again on the roadside banks this year, perhaps because farmers are spraying less.' As we sit to admire the view of the valley towards Newland she adds, 'A lot has changed even in the fairly short time we have been here. There were two dairy herds hereabouts, the cattle coming in to be milked twice a day. Now it's all gone except for a few sheep.'

Final tribute should be paid to the sheep, the Forest's most effective landscapers. While the legal rights of the sheep badgers remain a grey area, a stand-off between them and the authorities since the end of the last century permits the commoning of some five thousand sheep within the statutory Forest boundary

Blakeney sheep badger Henry Mills, with Meg.

Sling's annual sheep fair.

(see map). They may often be a nuisance on roads and in residential areas which fall within the Forest's limits, but keep down woodland undergrowth and trim roadside verges with unmatchable efficiency and cheapness. While some sheep badgers are neglectful, others such as Blakeney's Henry Mills (and sheepdog Meg) fuss over their flock as much as any of the 'proper' farmers who can be seen buying and selling their stock at Sling's annual August sheep fair.

CHAPTER 4

Health

At Drybrook's Quabbs House just before his retirement after thirty-five years as the village's GP, Dr Arthur Hooper sat in what used to be the surgery before the practice moved to new premises next to the village hall in 1991. 'In the early days we made up our own prescriptions here, chemist shops then being in short supply. In my previous practice in Weobley I used a pestle and mortar!

'We made a lot of home visits in those days as people did not have cars. You saw whole generations living together and in that way became a friend of the family. Today you have clinics which are much better equipped than we were, and far more preventive medicine, but the personal bond is not so strong these days. You were able to allow patients to talk – not for too long, though – so you could understand their real problems. Today the NHS is bedevilled by masses of paperwork and computers, so the clinical content of our work is less. During the war Dr Sumption was treating six thousand patients single-handed. Mind you, he was writing the prescription as they came in through the door!

'Before we came here people warned us, "They are a strange lot in the Forest of Dean", but we found them absolutely marvellous' adds his wife Pat. As with all GPs' wives in those days, before the advent of receptionists and practice managers, she was an essential part of the practice. The pair were delighted when their daughter Jane became the partnership's practice manager, thus continuing the family connection. Dr Hooper was also pleased he was being succeeded by a woman GP. 'It's a very definite advantage for women patients.' For the photograph he brings out an old Dr Cameron-style leather Gladstone bag. 'Nowadays I use an efficient black case with compartments for different instruments but I keep the brown bag to carry various medicines.'

Since retirement he has continued to be active in the Rotary Club, whose Royal Forest of Dean branch was formed in 1958. Over the years they have raised large sums which they have donated to a multitude of local good causes, including the Lydney and Dilke hospitals. 'The Club's first major project was the promotion of a centre to bring together facilities and services for three groups: the mentally or physically handicapped, and those disadvantaged people capable of working in sheltered employment,' explains Rotarian Brian East. 'The Forest of Dean Occupational Unit, Alpha Sheltered Workshops and Adult Training Centre, all now accommodated in Cinderford's Valley Road, opened in 1968.

'One of Rotary's most important projects was initiated in 1974 – the rebuilding and equipping of Lydney's old fire station in Victoria Road. The idea was to provide a place for the elderly and handicapped to meet, to have a luncheon club,

Dr Arthur Hooper putting away his GP's medicine bag after thirty-five years at Drybrook's The Quabbs.

and to allow the Lydney meals-on-wheels service to be extended into surrounding villages. The whole of the club became involved, every member being allocated to one or more of the committees, and each member's business and professional expertise being used to the advantage of the project. Many other local organisations gave their support, over £12,000 was raised, and the Victoria Centre was opened by Lady Bledisloe in 1977.'

An earlier Mrs Bathurst had founded the first of the Forest's pair of cottage hospitals almost a century previously. Herself paralysed, Mrs Mary Bathurst formed a fund-raising committee and launched charity events at Lydney Park later known as the 'Hospital Teas'. The committee leased a house at Aylburton, hired staff and recruited local citizens as subscribers. As its rules noted: 'A weekly contribution according to the ascertained means of the patients is required; but the hospital must, in a great measure, be supported by the donations and subscriptions of those more favourably circumstanced.'

By the new century Lydney was expanding so greatly that premises more convenient to the town and its industries, such as Richard Thomas's tinplate works, were required. The Bathursts provided land at the corner of their estate on the Bream Road, Richard Beaumont Thomas donated £1,000, and local people organized events such as dances, town hall concerts and parades marshalled by the Oddfellows and Ancient Order of Foresters. Opening in 1908 the new hospital soon after received an influx of First World War wounded. Charles Bathurst, the future first Viscount Bledisloe, became chairman of governors at the end of the war, serving until 1948 when the hospital became part of the National Health Service.

Arriving in Lydney after air force service as a Canadian volunteer, Dr Charles Carson was among a succession of local doctors who operated at the hospital as well as running their own practices. Dr James Brambell, who retired in 1972 after forty-two years here, was brother of *Steptoe and Son* actor Wilfred Brambell. Dr John Cardale, having arrived in the 1940s, retired in the 1980s. The idea of installing a plaque in the town hall in recognition of their services was proposed by parish council chairman and town pharmacist J.C. Hughes. The long-serving matron from 1924 up to her retirement in 1945 was Miss D.J. Gould. Miss A.M. Bawden succeeded her till her death in 1965.

On the death of Lord Bledisloe in 1958, town councillors and the Friends of Lydney Hospital fund-raising committee agreed to build a physiotherapy department in his memory. A generous donation by John Watts, head of the Lydney family's transport and motor accessories business, allowed work to begin in 1962. Having joined the Friends of Lydney Hospital committee, his nephew Melville Watts (also now a Verderer) became chairman of the trustees when it became a registered charity in 1979. Since then he has headed fund-raising efforts which have financed successive new facilities, such as the £72,000 for a new X-ray department which opened in 1995. In his speech on that occasion Christopher Bathurst, the present Lord Bledisloe, pointed out that, 'This is a truly magnificent achievement, especially when one remembers that only three years ago they also gave £120,000 for the new operating theatre.'

Outside Cinderford, the Dilke Memorial Hospital was built with the donations of a host of ordinary Foresters

Melville Watts, Verderer and Lydney cottage hospital fund-raiser since 1968.

Matron Joyce Coates in the week of her retirement after fifty years at the Dilke Memorial Hospital, with then manager Andrea Gallagher.

as well as of the 'great and good'. Launched to commemorate Charles Dilke, the Forest's MP from 1892 to 1911, it opened in 1923. New facilities added to the Dilke in 1994 included a women's wing, named after Mrs Joyce Coates who retired as matron that year after fifty years at the hospital.

Forest born and bred paediatrician Professor John Emery (eighty-three) achieved national and international eminence in his career at Sheffield University and children's hospital. His father, known as 'B.J.', was Aylburton's schoolmaster for forty years. 'I remember as a child Lord Bledisloe coming to visit my father in this house,' says John. 'They would spend hours together in the back room sorting out parish affairs. They drew up the constitution for the Memorial Hall, for example. Or Lord

Professor John Emery in front of old iron-workings in his Aylburton garden.

Bledisloe would practice one of his House of Lords speeches in which he used Aylburton agricultural projects as an example of what could be done to promote rural life elsewhere around Britain. The only trouble was that we children had to be very quiet on those occasions, which we didn't appreciate at all.'

After his father's schoolroom and Lydney grammar school, John went to Bristol University before getting a job as a medical academic at Sheffield. His wife Mytts, a history teacher, was a fellow student at Bristol. Their hobby is history and at Sheffield they were among those successful in safeguarding one of the city's old iron mills. He was introduced to historical research at an early age. Lord Bledisloe had invited Mortimer Wheeler to excavate Lydney Park's Roman temple and Norman castle, and Dr Scott-Garrett was digging at the Woolaston Roman villa. 'I used to know the latter's son. His father used to press-gang us into going down to help dig, though we managed to avoid the work as often as possible.' He was thinking of writing a history of the village. 'I can't just sit about here doing nothing. It's a good relaxation after so many years of producing papers on so many technical subjects.'

The throwaway phrase camouflages a lifetime's work which includes pioneering research into spina bifida and cot deaths. John was also a frequent expert witness in murder trials, his days in court being captured in a series of sketches in the sketchbooks he takes everywhere with him. Though he talks of his retirement, he hasn't ever fully retired. As Professor Emeritus, he keeps a house in Sheffield and goes into the hospital most days – spending weekends and holidays at Aylburton. When his father died at the age of ninety-six some fifteen years ago, John inherited the house, younger brother David and his wife living next door.

He leaps up from the patio to show us the caves at the back of the garden possibly dug by Roman iron miners. On rambles around the neighbourhood that summer he had discovered the remains of a watermill in the valley below Aylburton Common chapel. 'I was brought up here but never knew it existed,' he says delightedly. His neatly numbered sketchpads include portraits of colleagues from around the world he has sat with at innumerable conferences. Many of them were flying into Sheffield for a banquet that week to mark his eightieth birthday. There were also drawings of his grandchildren, several of whom were at that moment piling into the back of his daughter-in-law's estate wagon at the end of a weekend. How many grandchildren did he have? 'God knows! I leave it to my wife to keep track.'

George Gordon-Smith and his wife Sue came to the Forest twenty years ago, George having previously been an expedition leader in north and west Africa. 'It was mostly serious scientific stuff for the Swiss and German governments in places like the central Sahara. We went out there in 1969 but everything became progressively political. My parents were living at Goodrich, so we looked around for a place fairly near.' They found The Orchards, a pair of semi-detached cottages surrounded by a sixteen-acre smallholding at the top of the track climbing up past the former Stowfield hospital. It was, as it later turned out, an ideal place for a community for those with severe learning disabilities, such as their own daughter Helen.

When he came back from Africa George initially worked as export manager for a Newport firm, then started his own haulage business. When their daughter was born, she developed a cranial cyst. By the time it was diagnosed and operated on it had caused permanent brain damage. As George points out, 'Someone in that position may be mentally disabled but they are not necessarily stupid. Those who have suffered brain damage may be as intelligent as the rest of us.'

As Helen grew up, George and Sue looked around at the educational facilities available to her, and began to have doubts about the suitability of what was on offer. 'The education and health services were run by dedicated people but the approach was very much to provide a service – a school or sheltered workshop – and people had to accept the system. We and other parents increasingly thought it should be the other way around, that the provision should be user-led. You allow the individuals to make their choices as far as possible, and then create the services to match.'

He and others launched The Orchards Trust in 1988. 'Our only assets were a wooden shed and £30 we had collected in a tin box. When we looked for charitable funding we couldn't get any money. When we put it to the banks as a business proposition we got the money straight away. The original proposal was to provide three residential places and work for three people three days a week on the smallholding.' The availablity of finance is explained by the fact that all kind of remedial homes are much in demand, and cost a lot of money. In places like Kent, near to London's vast population, it can cost well over £1,000 a week per client. 'We cost less than that but we won't take people from outside the county. The severely disabled suffer enough problems without being taken away from their families and friends.'

The first step was to convert the cottage next to that occupied by George and family to accommodate the first three residents and live-in care staff. The shed became the smallholding's day centre. The Trust was established as a commercial charity with parents and others serving as trustees, George being employed as full-time administrator and any profits being ploughed back into the charity's funds. What happened next is slightly unclear, since the place you visit up the Stowfield track is a super-modern cluster of residences around central rooms and services. Even if unlimited funding had been provided, which it wasn't, it is incredible to see that such an extraordinary building was planned, built and then staffed in such a short space of time up till its opening in the early 1990s.

Offa's Dyke, as it is called, provides three four-bedroom bungalows for a dozen residents in need of total care, which requires a range of staff working through

George Gordon-Smith at his Orchards home for those with severe learning difficulties.

twenty-four hours on eight-hour shifts. The job of sorting out the finances and administration of such an operation is formidable, complicated by the consideration that each of the bungalows is encouraged to live as independently as possible. Each is provided with a minibus, so the quartet of residents plus their care staff can get out and about where and when they want. 'They may want to go ten-pin bowling, shopping in Gloucester or going to places like Lydney's Golden Triangle club. In winter, when it's more difficult to travel, there are places such as the Saturday club at Cinderford's Forest of Dean Centre. Some have built up connections with what you might call mainstream organizations. In Lydbrook itself the church and Silver Band have been very welcoming. One of our people takes part in amateur dramatics and is now in his third production.'

When we arrived, training manager David Miles said, 'George is somewhere around, because you can hear his raucous laugh'. While he is anxious to share credit with all the others involved in The Orchards creation, George is refreshingly robust in his attitude to professional jargon. 'I was at a meeting of quite senior people recently where they spent half an hour trying to decide what to call something in a politically correct manner. I totted up what their time had cost and it came to something like £400. What you call something isn't important, it's what you are doing that counts.'

At The Orchards this already included the day scheme for clients working on the smallholding. The public are invited to visit at weekends to buy what they produce, including bedding plants, vegetables and firewood. There is a detached home at Lydbrook's White House with three residents and a seven-strong staff team, who can use the Offa's Dyke facilities as and when they choose. An interesting addition is Ruardean Hill's Hilltop villa respite home, providing short-stay accommodation for five temporary residents (looked after by a staff of ten) whose usual carers are thus allowed a short break.

'In caring for the profoundly disabled you have to pay attention to the needs of the carers – family or professionals. It's bloody tough for the professionals even though they work a set number of hours and get their weekly days off and holidays. They sometimes get burned out, so imagine what it's like for the family carers, no time off, no training, no holidays.' With his usual matter-of-factness he adds laughingly, 'It also allows a holiday for those being looked after. They feel frustrations in their home life just like the rest of us, only they aren't able to get away from it quite so easily.'

CHAPTER 5

Transport

'I owe a lot to the railways,' says Mike Rees (sixty-three) at his perch in the office of Coleford's former railway goods shed. 'My Dad met Mum, then Maude Bartlett, as she waited on the Coleford platform to travel back to Parkend of an evening. He chatted her up from the engine and sometimes smuggled her on to the footplate for a ride. I then grew up in the middle of rivalry between the Forest's two railway companies. Grandad, George Ward Rees, lived next door to us in Lydney's Valley Road. He worked as a signal engineer with the Midland Railway, later the London, Midland and Scottish. Based at Lydney Town station, next to the level-crossing, he looked after the signal-boxes on the Berkeley to Parkend route, including the one serving the swing-bridge over the Gloucester–Sharpness Canal. He used to sit me on his knee and tell me stories of the bridge. Then I'd go back home and my father, who worked for the GWR, used to say, "Don't pay any attention to him. The Great Western knocks spots off the LMS – Late, Mucky and Slow!"'

Mike's great grandfather, David Rees, was fireman at Parkend's ironworks, keeping the great furnace going as far back as the 1860s. The family lived in the now demolished Barracks terrace overlooking the River Lyd. Mike's dad Victor started work at Lydney's Great Western Railway engine sheds in 1916, later becoming a fireman. 'He fired the last passenger train from Coleford in 1929. He was made a driver in 1936 and sent to Exeter until posted to Severn Tunnel Junction during the last war. He once drove an ammunition train through "the Hole" to Bristol. Stuck on a siding near Temple Meads he found himself in the middle of an air raid with bombs falling all around. He says his fireman was kneeling on the footplate, praying.'

Back at Lydney after the war Vic continued until it all closed down in 1964. Having run the last goods service from Lydney to Cinderford via Bullo, he retired but was to have a further spell on the footplate. As a founder member of the Dean Forest Railway he became its first driver from 1971 to 1976, training up others including his son. For, having a technical bent, Mike started out in the Lydney telegraph department in 1951. 'My main job was maintaining the old Wye Valley line signalling system, including the signal-boxes at Tintern and Monmouth. In 1959 I was posted to Cinderford station as signal and telegraph technician for the whole Forest and Wye Valley network until it closed five years later.'

Moving to Coleford, he started an electrical business, now run by his son Dave with Mike's continuing help as bookkeeper. In his spare time he was among those setting up the Dean Forest Railway, becoming its first chairman. It was then

Mike Rees at Coleford's old railway goods shed with his about-to-be-restored Peckett engine.

based at Parkend's former station, where his dad taught him to fire and drive a Peckett shunting engine on the short stretch of track. In 1986 he managed to buy the Coleford goods shed site where, over the years since, he has built up an unexpectedly large (given the building's small size) collection of railway material. As part of the clearance of the station site for the future supermarket and shopping centre, the goods shed was due to go. Organizing a petition, Mike and colleagues collected two-and-a-half thousand signatures over a single weekend and the district council relented.

He and fellow enthusiasts did the shed up, displayed objects saved when the lines closed, and installed a minature railway track around the perimeter to give children rides. He also acquired the magnificent 1906 vintage GWR wooden signal-box which stands next to the shed. 'It comes from the main line near Taunton. British Rail wanted to get rid of it – they were going to burn it down – so I enquired if I could buy it. They agreed to sell it for £5 if I moved it myself. It took eighteen months to get it ready for moving. Then BR closed the line for four hours one Sunday, and a giant crane lifted the box – sawn into two halves – on to transporter lorries.'

Reassembled at Coleford, it had to be completely refitted with signal levers, Lydbrook's Ian Jameson-Beale doing most of the work, while Milkwall's Fred Carmen looked after the woodwork. A peek at the machinery in the ground floor reveals an astonishing array of heavy metal and wires. 'It's a whole mechanical locking computer,' says Mike, adding that each signal lever has a counterbalance weighing a hundredweight. When you ask to have a go, Mike hands over the signalman's cloth, to prevent sweaty hands corroding the steel.

At the goods shed platform is a 1936 vintage Peckett engine which Mike rescued from a Horsham scrapyard after it had spent most of its working life at Ironbridge and Stourport power stations. Having had a feasibility survey carried out by Bill Parker's mechanics from the Flour Mill restoration workshop, he plans to restore it to working order and run it on the few short yards of track within his perimeter. At our departure he asks jovially, 'Don't you find that Bill Parker is, well, a bit eccentric?' Coming from someone dressed in railwayman's uniform and cap, this is a bit rich. It is certainly true though that railway enthusiasts undertake projects one would think impossible – the creation of the Norchard Railway Centre being the proof.

❖ ❖ ❖

Dougie Phelps (fifty-one), born at Wigpool, was a pipe fitter at one of Cinderford's firms serving traditional Forest industries but worked as a hobby at weekends for the newly formed Dean Forest Railway Preservation Society. Founded in 1970 when the Parkend to Lydney route was the last left open in the

Forest, the Society rented the old sidings area at Parkend. Pioneering members included Mike Rees and his father, Vic, and John Harris – known as 'Cuz' or 'J.R.' – a one-time train fireman at Lydney who had switched to lorry driving when steam ended in 1963.

'It was J.R. who bullied everyone into helping or giving and raising money,' says Dougie who, as a member from 1971, retains the membership number 316. 'Mike and Vic Rees, Dave Mundy and Lyn George arranged the purchase of the first locomotive, a little Peckett shunter from the Uskmouth power station in Newport. What John really wanted was a Great Western Railway engine, and in 1972 we bought 5541, a Prairie tank from the Barry scrapyard.' The nucleus of volunteers set about restoring the yard, opening the old goods shed as a small museum and re-laying two hundred feet of track. He recalls how a former permanent-way ganger Bill Poskett, living in the railside cottage next to Lydney parish church, located materials and helped with

Veteran mechanics of the Dean Forest Railway: Dougie Phelps (right), son Geoff (left) and the Norchard Railway Centre's chief mechanical engineer Phil Davies on the footplate.

restoring the track. The Society's first 'steam day' was in October 1971 when 'Uskmouth' hauled paying passengers in a brake van along what gained the Forest another *Guinness Book of Records* entry as the world's shortest passenger railway.

'We worked on the Prairie on Sunday afternoons, a bunch of amateurs who had never done anything like it before,' Dougie recalls. 'There was no cover, so in winter it was pretty rough. When it was finished and driven for the first time, the proper drivers went off to the Fountain to celebrate. So myself, Dick Maddicks, Dave Hall and Alan Gurner thought we would have a go. I've done all this work so I reckon I deserve it, I thought. Anyway, we managed to drive it down and back up the sidings.' British Rail was still using the branch line for carrying stone but the society was able to buy the former Norchard colliery site and the land of the one-time West Gloucestershire power station next to it. Arranging the paperwork and funding for all this was as formidable a task as the physical labour of restoration. First chairman of the Dean Forest Railway Limited Company set up to own and operate the railway was the late Peter Skinner. The Dean Forest Railway Society was established as the membership organization which is the company's largest shareholder and nominates two directors to the DFR board.

'The land at Norchard looked like natural forest, covered in scrub and bracken,' Dougie continues. 'We managed to get the Army Apprentices College at Beachley to use it for a land clearance exercise, so they came in with their bulldozers and diggers. We laid a couple of hundred yards of track, built a concrete platform and started steam days in 1978. It had a hill and a bend, so this made it much more exciting than Parkend.' Phil Davies (thirty-four) started working at the Norchard Centre around this time (with membership number 883). He had gained an interest in steam from his father who worked as a ship's engineer on ships sometimes sailing out of Avonmouth. Later, when working as a blacksmith, Phil used to come across the Severn Bridge on Friday evenings and return Sunday. 'Nightime I would find a brake van or wagon and doss down in a sleeping bag,' he recalls.

'They were just beginning to clear the space where the repair shed now stands but it took a long time to build and wasn't finished till 1990 – so we were still repairing the rolling stock outdoors. Even when it was ready it didn't have any overhead lifting gear, so we have to jack everything up to carry out work on it.' In these early 1980s John Harris, by now Chief Mechanical Engineer (or CME), located a sister engine to the GWR Prairie in Somerset. 'He was looking for a sucker to buy it and found me,' says Bill Parker (fifty), son of Stowe Grange's Oxford don William Parker. 'He is still at it, finding choice items and persuading someone – or a lot of people – to pay.'

When British Rail closed its Swindon works in 1986 Bill, a chartered surveyor, set up the Swindon Railway Workshop, owned by a charitable trust, to restore old steam engines. Phil Davies adds that it was Bill who, with Peter Skinner, used his surveyor's skills to negotiate the purchase of the branch line from British Rail back in 1981, and later set up the first Community Programme training scheme whose workers built the toilet and shower block at Norchard. Many others too numerous to mention were involved in extending the Norchard facilities: David Lyall was company solicitor from very early on and John White has handled the finances since 1981. The museum and shop block, the former canteen of the London

Rubber Company on Lydney's trading estate, was planned by Bernard Davies. The level-crossing at Lydney's Hill Street was replaced in 1987 by Trevor Radway and others when the line opened as far as Lydney Lakeside. In 1994 a level-crossing was built as part of the Lydney by-pass – the railway having an existing right of way from 1809 – and the Lydney Junction station and extensive sidings reopened with a signal box transported from Heysham. In 1997 the Railway made a great leap in its 'push to Parkend', reinstating the Whitecroft level-crossing and doubling the track at both Whitecroft and Parkend, giving the railway its own facilities in preparation for the reopening of passenger services.

Phil had meanwhile moved to the Forest and was working with the Grail's engineering firm at Steam Mills. Having been appointed the DFR's Chief Mechanical Engineer, with Dougie's son Geoff (thirty-five) as his deputy, Phil and Geoff thought of engine restoration as a full-time trade. They asked Bill Parker if they could hire his refurbished Flour Mill colliery engine house to work on a steam engine. Bill suggested instead they might work for his Swindon Railway Workshop at the Flour Mill. 'We didn't take long to say yes,' Phil relates. 'Since 1996 we have restored the working replicas of Brunel's Iron Duke and Stephenson's Rocket for York's National Railway Museum. We have three others in the works at the moment, including one more for York.' The workload was by now such that Dougie joined them in 1998.

❖ ❖ ❖

The Flour Mill colliery, which first mined coal in 1869 and became part of Princess Royal in 1908, was one of the many industrial sites occupying Bream's Oakwood valley – stone quarries, iron mines, collieries and even a blast furnace. The brick structure built in 1908 to house engines powering the mine's huge electric pumps has survived as one of the Forest's few handsome industrial buildings. Bill Parker bought it in 1993 as a home for Swindon Heritage Trust and restored it from semi-derelict condition, complete with overhead gantry crane under a magnificent boarded roof, suitable for repairing historic GWR steam locomotives. Its tall and wide wooden doors open on to a yard with rails running down to the route of David Mushet's Oakwood tramway built in 1825. With Forest Enterprise's approval the tunnels built over the tramway by the colliery are being repaired, and perhaps one day a coal mine headframe will once again be installed here.

Bill Parker at Bream's former Flour Mill colliery engine house, now a steam locomotive repair workshop.

Alec Pope, long-time Forest industrial heritage conservationist, photographer and archivist.

Despite living in the USA and working as a surveyor in the Americas and Eastern Europe, Bill has become what he dubs 'a buyer of last resort' of other historic but decrepit properties in the Forest. Already in hand is the refurbishment of Bream's New Inn, one of the Forest's oldest and finest residential buildings. Built by a Bristol merchant in the late sixteenth century and expanded in 1637 – the date carved on the mantlepiece of its open fireplace – it became a public house from Victorian times until 1962. Some years after it closed it was purchased by Melville Watts, living at the Priors Mesne great house outside Bream; he carried out major structural work before selling it to the Dean Heritage Centre as a possible ancilliary location to Soudley. This turned out not to fit in with the museum's plans and after many years on the market it was bought by Bill in 1995, with no specific plans for its eventual use. Restoration of the main wing has involved new floors, walls and ceilings, and the building and its grounds are becoming once again a visual asset to the village.

The greatest challenge Bill faces remains Gunn's Mill near Flaxley, the base of which is arguably Britain's oldest surviving 'complete' iron furnace. Built in the early 1600s when the Dean was centre of Britain's iron industry, it was rebuilt in 1682. Later a paper mill, taking advantage of the giant waterwheel, and then a farm and sawmill – as recalled by Ray Wright – the structure had been near to collapse for fifty years when Bill quixotically acquired it. 'Once the New Inn is finished we will see what we can do about it,' he says.

The founding of the Dean Heritage Centre was another Rotary Club initiative. Various local historians, notably Cinderford's Alec Pope, had collected objects from the Forest's industrial and transport past but there was no local museum to exhibit them in. Rotary's 1979 president Basil Johnson convened a public meeting which enthusiastically backed the idea of trying to launch one. A project team was formed to investigate possibilities, backed by the district council's planning chief Geoff Pyart. They looked around for a suitable building in an appropriate location and lighted upon what at first sight was an unpromising candidate. Soudley's Camp Mill was at the time leased as a car-breaker's scrapyard, a photograph in the museum's brochure showing its then dreadful state. The fortunate factor was that its owners, the Joiner family, were sympathetic to the museum idea. Thanks to their generosity it was made available to the trust formed in 1982 to hold the property and funds raised. The district council acquired surrounding land which they also handed over to the trust.

The first six trustees were, in addition to Basil as chairman, Elsie Olivey (secretary), John Joiner, Tom Walding, Gareth Jones and Diana Court, its board also including two representatives of the Friends of the Dean Heritage Museum Trust. Members of the Friends society undertook strenuous fund-raising events, including a sponsored walk around the Forest's statutory boundary, a total of fifty-five miles. Its first director, Richard Tampling, was appointed; an eighty strong Manpower Services Community Programme team was formed; and work began on the near derelict premises under the supervision of Tony Quinn, foreman of the Joiners' building firm. Almost incredibly, the mill was able to open in 1983, with the mill pond beside it re-excavated to form one of the Forest's most pleasant vistas.

The modern café block was built in the following year, also accommodating craft workshops and the 'Steam Power and Transport, 1800' gallery. Here is displayed the museum's single finest exhibit, a beam engine built in the nearby Hewlett foundry for Lightmoor colliery around 1830. When the mine closed in 1940 the machine was rescued and sent to the National Museum of Wales, who returned it to the Heritage Centre on permanent loan. Restored to working order by Alec Pope, its moving parts are today powered by electricity.

In 1986 David Mullin became director and new trustees were appointed. Countryside ranger in these early years was Mike Pratt who pioneered activities such as the charcoal burn on the hillside above the Soudley Brook. Twice a year, since the ranger post disappeared, volunteers tend the stack, sleeping beside it overnight to ensure the fire does not burn through the turf covering. The ton of charcoal produced is sold to contribute towards museum funds.

This ancient craft, the basis of the Forest's iron industry, served the forge built here early in the seventeenth century. Charles II ordered its demolition as part of the programme to restore the Forest's timber production for naval shipbuilding. The site reverted to its rustic tranquillity until the nineteenth century and the building of the Cinderford to Bullo Pill tramroad. Quantities of tram plates were made by Samuel Hewlett at his foundry, some of his rails, wagon wheels and mileposts being displayed in the gallery next to his Lightmoor beam engine. The present fine stone building was erected as a corn mill in 1876. From 1888 it was a leatherboard mill until 1911 when it became a sawmill. After 1952 it was a piggery and then scrapyard.

Major building works in the late 1980s aided by Rural Development Commission grants doubled the gallery space, added the visitor entrance and souvenir shop, and created the dam-top walkway. Ian Standing, Coleford's well-known dentist and assiduous local historian, switched careers to become the museum's curator in 1988 (and director in 1990) with the job of creating new displays from the material donated by Foresters. It is a place for an extended visit – or visits. In addition to the galleries illustrating all aspects of Forest life, there is the recreated Forester's cottage out the back, complete with a pigscot occupied by a Gloucester Old Spot sow.

Former Dean Heritage Centre director David Evans and curator Sarah Finch above the Camp Mill millpond.

From the car park three nature trails wend through Foundry Wood, Bradley Wood and around the Soudley Ponds. On the hillside is the Zion chapel which, since its closure in 1992, has been on lease to the museum. Inside the café block are the workshops such as that of blacksmith Graham Tyler who welds traditional and modern ironwork as well as creating his metal sculptures. A further attraction is the Gage Library, its core collection of old books and maps bequeathed by Laurie Gage, an antiquarian bookseller who developed an interest in the Forest and Gloucestershire.

Ian Standing moved on to become founding curator of Ross-on-Wye's Heritage Centre in the town's old Market House, and is now Community Heritage officer for the reconstituted Herefordshire County Council. He was succeeded at Camp Mill by David Evans (thirty-three) as director and Sarah Finch (twenty-eight) as curator, (David moving on in 1998). You imagine what it must have looked like to Vic Rees as he passed by on that last steam train journey from Cinderford in 1969.

Forest railway passenger services were largely superseded in post-First World War years by coaches. Having served as motor-engineers during the First World War, brothers John and Arthur Watts bought army surplus lorries from Salonika which they did up at their Lydney garage. Some they sold on, others they converted to early omnibuses, serving the Welsh valleys from 1921 and the Forest in the following year. Having formed with other 'Big Six' operators the Red & White company, they also expanded into the other vehicle businesses today making up Watts of Lydney. Of Arthur's three sons, Geoffrey was chairman of the separate United Transport company in the early 1990s, with fifty thousand employees worldwide. Cecil concentrated on the Watts Tyre & Rubber Co., while twin Melville was managing director of the holding company and, as seen above, fund-raiser for Lydney hospital.

Starting out in Cinderford at the same time as the Watts in Lydney were the Grindles of Woodside Street, where their original stables are still marked by a couple of garages – one with antique fuel pumps on its forecourt. In the last century William Grindle ran a fuel merchant's business, using horse-drawn carts for his paraffin and coal deliveries. He also provided horses for ceremonial occasions; black for funerals, white for weddings. Son Harry developed the business until being called up for the war, during which he served in the 13th Gloucestershire Regiment. Although still at school his sons Percy and Roy helped their mother carry on.

In postwar years the brothers, like the Watts, acquired ex-War Department lorries. Percy started in 1926 with a Dodge. Going his own way, Roy later bought the yard behind the Swan Hotel as his depot. During the week the lorries carried freight. Having bolted on benches, Percy also ferried miners between the town and outlying pits. In 1930 the custom-built coach was introduced and the brothers offered leisure trips around the area. There were popular evening 'Mystery Tours' (at 1s 6d) and Sunday trips to Rodley Sands – not without some rivalry.

Roy applied for the renewal of his licence for the route, which his father had served with horse and cart. It was opposed by the council because of the narrowness of the lane but eventually duly renewed. As the newspaper report of the hearing before the Western Area Traffic Commissioners continues: 'A similar application was made by Mr P. Grindle, the brother of the first applicant, the latter opposing it.' There were excursions further afield, to Cardiff and Barry Island, and the 'Lovers' Special' into Cheltenham of a Sunday evening. 'In the 1920s and 1930s most girls in the Forest went away to domestic service,' explains Percy's daughter Norma. 'On Sunday evenings the young men, mostly colliers, would pile into the coach to visit their sweethearts who also had Sunday afternoons off.'

When Grindles started continental tours in the 1950s, their coaches were lifted on to the cross-Channel ferries by crane.

Third generation of Forest coach owners, Harry Grindle (foreground) with (from left) cousins Gerald, Norma with husband Jack Denton, and Michael at their Cinderford garage.

During the Second World War Roy had the contract to transport the workers to and from the munitions factories at Brickworth. The Tilling Stevens, a Lion and the wooden-slatted seated Bedfords were a familiar sight. When parked up at night they stretched along Woodside Street end to end, also filling Flaxley Street and Forest Road. 'You couldn't get spares so they were always breaking down and very difficult to start, which was still by an arm-wrenching starter handle. So some of the coaches would be left with their engine running all night, so they could tow the others to where they could start by rolling downhill,' says Norma.

Well-known drivers in those days were Eskey Bennett, Cyril Watkins, Jack Gardner, Tom Barnard and Briggan Young. The conductresses bus-hopped along the route, collecting fares on several buses. Among them were Alma Brookbanks, Barbara Grindle and Alice Wearing. 'Roy's sister Roma was among those helping out as a driver. Staff were so short that grandfather Harry was taught to drive at the age of sixty-five. He was a slow driver, which annoyed the workers wanting to get home for their tea. They used to throw rivets at him, which they carried in their pockets, to make him go faster. At the end of each journey the bus was always full of them.'

After the war Roy changed the grey/green colours to orange and lemon. In 1949 he began the extended holiday tours such as the eight-day tour to Scotland (at 14 guineas). In 1952 he was doing trips abroad, the coach being lifted by crane on to the Dover–Boulogne ferry. Roy's son Harry was by now in the business, becoming a feature in the schedules of many Forest institutions doing trips around and outside Britain. After driving the Forest of Dean Youth Band on twelve tours abroad they gave him a cup. Percy's wedding and funeral transport business with a fleet of vintage cars was taken over by son Gerald, who lives next to his sister Norma, whose husband Jack Denton had joined the firm as a driver in 1948. She and other brother Michael were also on the payroll.

Harry and his son Philip sold their business to Warners of Tewkesbury. Philip then took over the other side of the family's business – 'to carry on the family name', he explained. Today it owns six DAFs mostly engaged in school contracts and tours. While Harry is officially retired, the previous week he had been in Italy as a relief driver. At the depot off Valley Road he proudly showed off his pride and joy, the Bedford Val 70 Plaxton Panorama Elite six-wheeler he bought in 1972 but had long since been sold. Driving on the other side of the Severn a few years ago he spotted it and rebought it. Immaculately restored it is nowadays a regular sight at rallies such as the Speech House Steam Fayre.

CHAPTER 6

Shopkeepers

The ferrules requested by my carpenter to repair the legs of a wheeled trolley were to be found nowhere in London. On Coleford's Market Square the following week there was a sign reading: 'Ferules' (sic). It also offered:

Lighters
Pouches
Shaving requests
Walking sticks
Pipes
Tobacco
Loose tobacco
Batteries

'Not half-inch ferrules, I need three-quarter inch ferrules,' said the carpenter back in London. In Coleford another week later, Pat Bolter (sixty-one) – tobacconist, confectioner and barber – swapped ferrules. As well as performing a cut-price haircut, he produced from albums in his back room a photograph of the shop in the days of his father and grandfather. It has changed little today, despite the windows being bashed in from time to time by weekend revellers. Someone came around recently and stuck plastic over the old signs advertising Star and Player's cigarettes. 'I protested but he said that under new European regulations it was now illegal to advertise tobacco without a health warning underneath. It was only when I found out that the Square is a conservation area and no exterior alterations can be made without planning permission that he peeled them off again.'

Pat started as a barber helping out his dad while a youngster, taking over the shop full time in the 1960s. His oldest customer, whom he now visits at home, is ninety-one. His youngest are skinheads who, he says, 'want the whole lot off'. As he snips away early morning he casts an alert eye through the pane between barber shop and the front counter. 'Some of the schoolkids come in and try and nick things.' He relaxes when at 9 a.m. Julie, one of the four girls working here part time, arrives.

'We sell a lot of things – postcards, confectionery, habadashery, pipes and walking sticks. We also do umbrella repairs and sell ferrules to people making their own walking sticks.' On the shelves behind the counter ten jars of pipe tobacco are labelled with fragrant names such as Blackberry, Continental Gold,

Pat Bolter in front of the Coleford barber's and confectioner's shop formerly run by (below) his father, grandfather and aunt.

Tropical and Dunbar Original. Among uncharged-for services is a chat about what's happening in the town, how many late-night revellers were arrested by the police last Saturday night, and the occasional glimpse into distant local history.

Back in his barber's chair on another occasion I mention the Pace murder – or alleged murder – of the 1930s. Sheep badger and wife-beater Mr Pace of Sling died of a suspiciously large accumulation of arsenic. His wife was tried for murder in a case at Gloucester assizes which made national headlines. The jury acquitted her, choosing to accept the defence case that he absorbed the arsenic while dipping sheep rather than from increasing doses in his tea. Having sold her life story to a popular Sunday newspaper, she was driven to a South Coast hotel by a chauffeur employed by the paper. She married him shortly after and returned to the Forest where she led a quiet life thereafter. 'My dad was on the jury,' Pat casually remarks. 'He reckoned it was a scandal.' Did his dad think it had been a miscarriage of justice and the widow Pace should have been hanged after all? 'No, but he was six weeks off work without any pay.'

On the other side of the former church tower Keith Morgan (fifty-five) took on the barber shop from Mr Reg Wilce, whose original shop was a short distance away on the Gloucester Road. In his youth Keith helped out in the shop on Saturday mornings but worked most of his early life at Rank Xerox before taking on the shop in the late 1980s. In his leisure time he played in the Stompers jazz band. He also wrote poetry in Forest dialect published in two volumes by Coleford bookseller and folk musician Doug McLean. *The 'Azard o' Chimmuck Szwippin* (*The Dangers of Chimney Sweeping*) appeared in 1979, after which Keith was a popular performer of his verse at clubs around the Forest.

A second volume took its title from his hilarious poem 'Albert's Dree Wi'ker' (1985), describing how Albert managed to keep a bonfire going for a whole three weeks to the annoyance of his family and everyone else around. It ends with the epic stanza:

> Im loi there in 'is deckchair
> reflectin' on his pile,
> An reckoned ta 'iself as thic
> were best 'n by a mile.
> A dree wi'ker 'im 'ad managed
> ver the vurst time in 'is life,
> Despite loosin' all 'is neighbours,
> 'is whipput an' 'is wife.

On the White Hart side of Coleford's market place Mary Collis is speedily covering up a nude dummy in the Voluntary Social Aid shop window. 'We don't want people to get the wrong idea,' she explains as the Revd Gordon Johnson and his volunteer colleagues are photographed in front of it. Gordon (eighty-eight) opened the shop when he retired to the Forest with his wife, née Dix, from Christchurch. Other shops with the same name at Lydney, Ross and Chepstow are vestiges of a one-time secondhand clothes empire, for the Revd Johnson is

Coleford's other barber Keith Morgan. He is seen (below) as a two-year-old at a VE Day party at the former Lamb and Flag on the Gloucester Road, on the extreme left in the second row.

The Man Who Invented Charity Shops. Over five thousand of these now occupy prime sites in Britain's shopping streets, raising something like £300 million a year for the various charities who run them.

At their home towards the end of an English Bicknor lane, Gordon mildly comments on the situation back in the early 1960s. 'Oxfam wasn't too keen on the idea of dealing in old clothes but we gave them the shop we had started in Cambridge – and they now have six hundred or so around the country which provide them with almost a quarter of their overall income.'

A Yorkshireman, he studied theology at King's College, London. When the last war broke out he naturally joined the KOYLIs, the King's Own Yorkshire Light Infantry. Having spent what he describes as 'the most ghastly winter I can remember' in East Anglia during the months of the Phoney War, he was tempted by a circular which came around asking for volunteers for SOE – the Special Operatives Executive – which Churchill had set up with the aim of 'setting Europe alight'.

'Anything would be better than this, I thought, so I signed up. It was nothing really spectacular. I went on an expedition to Yugoslavia to meet up with Tito. When I was wounded in 1943 I wrote to the Bishop of Gloucester asking if he might possibly find me a church posting. He invited me to meet him at the Athaeneum Club in London. He was as deaf as a post and bawling these questions at me in the foyer. I expected him to say I would have to go to such and such a college to prepare for the ministry. Instead he asked if I could be ready for ordination in three weeks' time.

'I managed it and became curate at St Stephen's in Gloucester's Bristol Road. It turned out the previous curate had been sent as chaplain to the Queen Mother, Queen Mary, so they needed a replacement very quickly.' It was here that he met his future wife. ('I didn't have much choice in the matter,' he chuckles, talking about their eventual marriage.) He took up a curacy in north Yorkshire but found it too quiet a life 'and anyway I wanted to go back overseas. So I applied to rejoin the army and in 1954 they sent me as a chaplain to Westphalia in Germany, a beautiful country. Then it was to Berlin, which was a marvellous place. It was before the Wall went up, though, and there were thousands of refugees arriving from the east each week. Back in the UK I landed up at Tidworth on Salisbury Plain, which was an awful place, so I went as a vicar to Essex.'

Here, and in surrounding counties, he was asked to speak about Europe's refugee problem and thus became involved in the fledgling Oxfam. 'A group of Oxfam women in Cambridge were planning a fund-raising jumble sale but found the Guildhall was already booked. I had noticed an empty shop nearby, with a sign it was up for sale or rent, so I arranged with the agents we could take it over for a while. We piled everything inside and offered it for sale. At the end of three weeks we had made more than from any jumble sale. The other thing was we ended up with more stuff than we had started off with, because people kept bringing it in.

'So we opened another shop in Colchester which was just as successful. We knew some people in Rusholme in Manchester, a rough area of the city, but the one we opened there was successful as well. I told the people running it that if people came in who couldn't afford anything, they should be given the clothes free. There were also kids without shoes, and since we didn't want to damage their feet with

The man who invented charity shops: Revd Gordon Johnson and helpers at their Coleford shop.

secondhand shoes we bought them new ones.' The profits were distributed among various charities. 'Sue Ryder came to see me to ask how to raise money and I said, "Have you tried shops?" She hadn't, so we gave her the Rusholme shop and another in Tottenham, and handed over the Cambridge shop to Oxfam.'

By 1970 Gordon was a vicar in Cambridgeshire but travelling 1,500 miles a week visiting the shops. The organization was by now the registered charity Help for the Needy – the Society for Aid to the Hungry and Needy. As an office they bought an old farmhouse in Peterborough for £10,000 and did it up. 'Things got so busy that I had to give up either the charity work or the parish. Life in a country parish wasn't quite my line anyway, so I concentrated on the charity and kept my hand in as an honorary curate in London at weekends.

'My wife was a teacher, which made it possible for me to continue, since I was only being paid travelling expenses. When I reached retirement age and qualified for a pension my wife said she couldn't live without her trees, so we came here.' He was until recently an honorary curate at Lydbrook and then at a parish on the other side of Ross. Though finding it increasingly difficult to get around he visits the Coleford shop at least once a week. 'The one thing we can't get enough of is men's clothes,' he sighs.

Round the corner in Coleford's St John's Street is the Forest Bookshop launched by Douglas McLean (fifty-seven) in the Old Wine Vaults opposite in 1976. A

London Scot, he left school at fifteen. The son of professional musicians, he had been brought up by his grandparents – his grandfather being a well-known left-wing politician and newspaper editor. 'I was a school dropout. I'd failed the 11+ and become disillusioned with the educational system as it then was, so I left as soon as possible. But I loved reading and started to educate myself, encouraged by my grandfather.'

His first job was in a London bookshop for seven years, where he gained bookselling qualifications from evening classes. He then worked for a London publisher until he was offered a publishing post covering the south-west, Doug and family moving to Coleford in 1970. 'The job left little time for family and friends, so although we by now had three small children I decided to drop out and start a bookshop. I had hardly any capital but a lot of friends in the trade, and they helped me out with extended credit, shelving and suchlike. Quite a few people warned me, "A bookshop in the Forest? It will never work!" But Foresters are like their Welsh neighbours, very keen on their heritage and self-improvement, so it went well from the start.'

As well as selling books, Doug found himself publishing them. 'People brought me manuscripts to read and asked if I could suggest possible publishers. Since they were mostly on local subjects it seemed logical to do it myself.' The result was a sequence of books which represent a lot of the Forest's diversity, from industrial archaeology and memoirs of times past to poetry and walking guides.

As well as Ray Wright's *Secret Forest* (1980) and Keith Morgan's dialect poetry mentioned above (1979 and 1985), he put into print the bundle of poems Joyce Latham pushed through the shop letterbox. Her *Puzzle Wood* was followed by *Poems of a Forester* (1991). The late Dr Bill Tandy wrote his delightful reminiscences of *A Doctor in the Forest* (1978) and of his earlier years in India in *The Ever-Rolling Stream*. David Bick wrote of *The Old Industries of Dean* (1980) and Ralph Anstis *The Story of Parkend* (1982). Basil Lane, retired captain of an oil tanker sailing between Avonmouth and upriver towns, put his memories – and old photographs – into *Severn Tanking* (1991) and *Time and Tide Wait for No Man* (1993). A series of walking and pub guides by Jon and Heather Hurley included titles such as *Forest of Dean Pubs* and *Wyedean Walks*, several reprinted in updated editions. He also resurrected the work of the poet of the First World War, F.W. (Will) Harvey with a volume titled *Collected Poems, 1912–1957*.

Doug, too, acted as literary midwife, encouraging Winifred Foley to follow up her bestselling *Child of the Forest* (1974) with a second collection of childhood memories published as *No Pipe Dreams for Father* (1977). He also arranged the sale of the rights to these and a third volume, *Back to the Forest*, to the Oxford University Press who publish them together as *The Forest Trilogy* (1992). He introduced Joyce Latham to Stroud's Sutton Publishing, the result being her enormously successful memoirs *Where I Belong* (1993). Launch parties at the shop for local authors such as Coleford's Edna Healey, children's author and illustrator Shoo Rayner, Ralph Anstis and Andrew Taylor have become regular events.

Throughout his life Doug has played various musical instruments and for years performed as folk musician and composer with the group 'Something Stirred', including Chas and Jan Bayliss. He also went out with his guitar to local schools,

Coleford bookseller Doug McLean playing banjo and telling stories at the English Bicknor primary school.

storytelling with music to encourage an interest in reading. He recalls that the Forest's other bookseller, Tony Jones of the Lydney bookshop, used to come to buy books before he had his own business. 'He read *The Bookseller* each week and often knew what was coming out even before I did.'

Through meeting his second wife Lyn, who had strong links with the deaf community, he developed an interest in sign language and enrolled on a four-year course to learn it himself. 'In 1988 I went on to study for an Open University degree in deafness and deaf issues but found the necessary books were hard to come by. Since I was a bookseller I began gathering books and other materials for this market. I also started a mail-order catalogue which didn't just list books but gave appreciations by Lyn and myself. We now send out 50,000 copies three times a year to clients worldwide. A lot of foreign universities use us as their main supplier of books on deafness and we are beginning to produce our own audio-visual cassettes.' Distribution is handled by a staff of ten working out of a warehouse on the Mushet industrial estate, and in the bookshop itself you

Former art teacher Phyllis Lewis in her Bream craftshop studio sculpting one of her clay models.

sometimes see Doug conversing in sign language with visitors from around Britain and abroad. 'They say they have been buying books from us for so many years they wanted to come and meet us.'

'It's a dream come true,' says Phyllis Lewis (sixty-three) of the gallery she opened in Bream in 1996 at the back of the Farmer & Clark insurance office. 'I can now display not only my own models but also the work of so many talented artists and craftspeople from around the Forest.' Born in Broadwell, she moved to Bream in 1946 and lived in a cottage near the Princess Royal mine. Her grandfather was a collier and her mother, when small, used to accompany him to the level with a dilly box on her back.

At Bream's girls school she gained a scholarship to the grammar school but her parents couldn't afford it. So she went straight to work at the stonemason's at Cannop Ponds. 'I loved to watch the old masons carving gravestones and became fascinated with the idea of sculpting. But I also caught pleurisy from having to bike to work in the rain and suffering in wet clothes all day, which developed into tuberculosis.' She was at home for two years, her mother struggling to look after her, after which she worked at Beecham's for fourteen years.

At her mother's suggestion she then tried for art school, applying to what was then the Gloucester College of Art. 'The problem was that I was in my thirties with no portfolio of work to show. I begged my way in. I told the tutor, "I've waited so long you've got to accept me". He did but years later he told me he'd stayed up all night worrying whether or not to accept me.' Given a project to depict her native environment in any art form, she chose to model in clay, which has been her favoured medium ever since. It began the series of characters that by now have covered all aspects of the old Forest.

'The way of life was dying out and I wanted to catch it before it was all gone. The accent was going too. Ay lorst my 'un, but bein' a teacher you'm got to speak proper like. Well, I might 'ave got it back a bit since I retired. They used to discourage accents at school – hammer it out of you. Now they are encouraging the use of it in drama and writing.' After art school she went to Gloucester College of Education and then to Cheltenham's St Mary's where she gained a BEd Hons. For fourteen years thereafter she taught ceramics at Wyedean school. 'Her pupils thought she was wonderful,' adds Brian Clark. 'Quite a few talents have grown from her teaching.'

In retirement she concentrated on her models, fired in her high temperature kiln to become stoneware and glazed with earthy colours such as greys, blacks and brown. She has sold a lot, many of them specially commissioned. A simple figure taking a week to carve costs around £200. More complicated groups involving weeks of work are upwards of £600. One of her favourites was that commissioned by Harry Kear, of his great-grandmother bread-baking in the range oven of her Yorkley cottage.

The Forest of Dean Gallery and Craft Workshop having been made available by Brian Clark, she is able to work there during its Tuesday to Sunday opening hours. Paintings by Lydney's Jean Morgan, conductor of the Springfield Singers, adorn the walls. On display are woodcarvings by former policeman David Reynolds of Harrow Hill who took up the craft after a serious accident. There are the candles made by Doug Isles from the beeswax of the Hudnalls Apiaries at St Briavels. Retired teacher Joy Simpson of Primrose Hill makes wallhangings of Forest wool. Gerald Powles is a retired metal worker who casts items at his Sling workshop. Also from Sling, potter Amanda Smith shows her plates and dishes. All these are within a setting whose walls are decorated with local scenes by Graham Wilde, Wyedean's head of art and design and technology.

An example of Phyllis Lewis' work. One of her personal favourites: Harry Kear's great-grandmother baking bread in her Yorkley cottage.

CHAPTER 7

Church and Chapel

Bearded and bespectacled, in dog collar on this weekday morning and with pipe resting on his study table piled high with books, the Revd David Addison is the image of a Victorian country clergyman. Appropriately so, for he is vicar of Newlands' venerable All Saints, the 'cathedral of the Forest'. Living at Bisley near Stroud, he was honorary curate there – 'before it became Jilly Cooper's village'. He sighs with relief; 'I felt the need for a change having been in charge since setting up the department. The person who does the charismatic and argumentative bit is not necessarily the right person to consolidate an organization. At the same time I was looking after the parish during an interregnum and didn't want it to become permanent. I talked with Bishop Robert of Tewkesbury and he said there was a difficult parish in the Forest of Dean that needed attention.'

Newland already included the Redbrook church and was being combined with Clearwell. 'The All Saints interior was in bad condition. Redbrook church was going to be pulled down, and Clearwell parish covers Sling and Milkwall which are more part of Coleford. In retrospect it might not have been such a good idea to combine the two.' But David agreed to take it on in partnership with his wife Joy as deacon.

While born into the trade as son of a Suffolk clergyman, he was not initially much interested in religion. He studied fine art at Newcastle University and back home met one of his father's parishioners – the exceptionally young head of a local primary school. They married, David took a DipEd, and the couple moved to Leeds where he taught at the grammar school. He then decided to go to theological college. 'The bishop told me that with my views there were only two places in the country that would accept me. Wells took me on and I was ordained there.

'Myself and some other fellow students there were very interested in the worker-priest movement in France. The idea was that you should be in the world, not separate. So instead of going to a parish I went into Bradford museum's schools service. There was a lot of outreach work, so I was involved with trade unions, Probus clubs and the Asian community which was then becoming an important element in the city. We set up events where the incomers and the host population could meet and hopefully understand each other better.' His wife was teaching in a tough middle school while bringing up their three children, David also acting as honorary curate at local churches.

'The cathedral of the Forest', Newland's All Saints, with the Revd David Addison and cat.

When Cheltenham launched its own museums service after the 1974 local government reorganization, David moved south to become the head of the department. 'We started from scratch in an ex-library and gradually built things up. One success was persuading the council to buy Holst's former house which, with his widow Imogen Holst's assistance, became a study centre for his works, as well as a house visited by school parties for its period interior.' The Pump Room was developed into a heritage and events location and in 1980 he even managed to acquire a former pub as his office.

Taking us on a tour of All Saints he points out how the interior has been cleared to allow varied usage. 'In medieval times the philosophy was that the church was a public place, up to the chancel steps where the rood screen would once have marked off the inner sanctuary.' He talks with enthusiasm of the music festivals held here and of the successful restorations of the fabric and stained-glass windows. Having gained an MA in art history studying part time, he went on to gain a DLitt with a thesis on 'Picture collecting in Bristol and Gloucestershire, 1800–1860'. He teaches art history classes at the Dean College, while Joy teaches special needs pupils at the Lakers School. 'In the present day we have lost so much of what used to be a common culture that one of the ways of teaching religion is through paintings – as it was in the old days by images such as those in the stained glass windows.'

Of his role within the parish David says, 'Some people expect an old-style vicar who is here, there and everywhere – serving on every committee and being deferred to. I see my role more as an enabler, encouraging others to participate and contribute.' He talks with enthusiasm of how vergers, sidesmen, a tower keeper and a host of others keep All Saints running, and of how the Redbrook congregation was organizing all sorts of initiatives. At the same time he was keen on preserving the panoply of old-style services: 'Processions, gowns, *smells*! – they provide a historical continuity with the Church's past, a reminder of its roots.'

❖ ❖ ❖

In jeans and singlet with a little cross dangling around his neck, the Revd Cliff Davies (fifty-six) was in more contemporary vicar's garb as he perched on the wall of his Ruardean St John the Baptist churchyard. His great-grandfather, grandfather, father and himself were born in the village, where he now lives opposite the church in a modern bungalow vicarage next to the Old Rectory. One admires the great tower and spire of fourteenth-century origins and the twelfth-century chapel that was the first church, with the valley-top graveyard around it. 'It looks lovely in summer,' Cliff agrees. 'It is less attractive when you are conducting a burial service in winter.'

Former boxer, rugbyman and journalist, the Revd Cliff Davies at Ruardean's St John the Baptist.

Vicar since 1986 Cliff's path to the ministry was somewhat unusual. While a churchgoer in youth, he 'lapsed off' in his teens. A famous local sportsman, he was a boxer at fourteen – surviving bouts in the Gloucester boxing booths unblemished – and a formidable rugby player for the Drybrook team. After school and a couple of years as a cub reporter on the *Dean Forest Mercury*, he moved to the Cinderford office of *The Citizen*. 'For twenty-six years I covered the usual jobs of a local reporter: council meetings, courts, news stories and sport. I loved it all.' But, covering Saturday games for his job, he had to give up as a player.

Instead he became a Drybrook Rugby Club committee member and, since 1986, its immensely popular president. He was also able to continue his hobby of falconry which he had taken up in his teens. He exercises his two hawks in the field below the church, swinging the bait on the end of a cord as seen in the film *Kes*. He also continued as a member of Drybrook's pigeon club, whose birds are collected in baskets from a Nissen hut next to the rugby club each Friday evening during the racing season. Members adjourn afterwards to the club bar where you find that Drybrook harbours two national figures of the pigeon world. Local builder John James (sixty-five), retiring from business after an accident in 1975, had progressed from President of the Gloucestershire Federation to national president of the Royal Pigeon Racing Association for three years in the early 1990s (having, by the by, founded the Drybrook club as an eleven-year-old). Also at the table is Edward Camilleri who, somewhat ironically, lives in the Ruardean Old Rectory. A former army major and then town clerk for Bude in Cornwall, he was now the RPRA's general manager at its national headquarters in Gloucester.

It doesn't seem at all incongruous to listen to Cliff talking in such surroundings, pint in hand, about his rediscovery of faith. Well actually it does, but he has the relaxed *gravitas* to make it feel natural. Surely a few rugby club members couldn't resist the temptation to make a few cracks when he began to study for ordination? 'No, they knew I was serious about it and everyone was very supportive. When I took our four-year-old along to Sunday school it all came back. In the 1970s I seriously thought of joining the ministry but threw it aside for several years. In 1979 I had a word with the wife and she had already sensed what I wanted to do.'

In 1980 he trained at the Gloucester School of Ministry for three years while carrying on his day job. Ordained a deacon and a year later as priest, he became non-stipendary curate at Drybrook's Holy Trinity – 'the Forest church'. In 1986 he applied for the vacant chaplaincy of Ruardean (the term may not be technically correct but former fine distinctions between rectors, vicars, priests-in-charge and suchlike are nowadays mostly irrelevant). 'Me and the wife had a chat with the bishop and, after he had thought about it, he offered me the living. I was very lucky: it's a little bit unique for someone to be installed in their own home village and as far as I'm concerned this is the best part of the best country in the world.'

The job includes among other things the chairmanship of the governors of Ruardean's C of E village school, to which he has added the similar post for the Dean Hall School for those with learning disabilities next to the Speech House. 'The main job is to be seen around the village and to be seen to be approachable. People meet you in the street and ask if they can come and have a chat. Usually they want to talk about family problems – very rarely, incidentally, about marital problems. Whether they are regular churchgoers or not – or if they are of other denominations or religions – everyone is treated the same. Even if they never go through the door of the church, most people have a spiritual awareness. We are not a godless society.'

On the other side of the Forest at St Briavels, the Revd Pat Pinkerton had put the cat among the pigeons (in a manner of speaking) by becoming one of the first women to be ordained as priest in the Church of England. Some of the St Mary's parishioners were hostile to the idea. Yet when the parish lost its former vicar in 1991, the majority chose her as their incumbent, even though at that time she was only a deacon in Church of England terms.

Swirling into her modern rectory house in a close on the far side of the green from the church beyond the castle, Pat apologizes for being a bit late. She had been held up by someone seeking help. 'There are frequently occasions when you have your day planned out very efficiently – visits, meetings and suchlike – then someone comes to your door very distressed. You can't say, "Sorry mate, I'm off". My attitude is that they are all parishioners and that the church is there for everyone. People need to know that the church is there at difficult times in their life. There is no point in being in the ministry if I can't give people whatever help I can.

'Some people resent this, thinking the church ought to belong to those that are loyal to the church year in year out. I see it more as a constant process of bridge building with those who may not be regular attenders. In the old days there used to be the situation whereby people tugged their forelock to the local vicar. We are now off our pedestal I'm glad to say.'

In 1962 she went to the USA to work as a nurse. Suffering a back injury, she was forced to give up nursing. In a mildly curious echo of David Addison's experience she explains, 'I went to university to study art history and medieval church history. For my master's degree my subject was Benedictine monasticism and St Augustine's abbey at Canterbury in particular. I was a regular churchgoer anyway and was asked if I would consider studying for holy orders. It was a time of great uncertainty and pain. I am not a feminist by any means and having been brought up in the English tradition I didn't think women were worth very much in the Anglican church.

'Having been sent back to rethink my vocation, a year later I felt I had been called to be a priest. In 1982 I was the first woman to be ordained as priest in the El Camino Real diocese and was appointed a vicar. On a visit to England in 1985 I talked to three deaconesses and was very upset by the attitude of many in the Church of England. There was no concept of the ministry of the laity. The American church was ten years ahead. I thought, "Here I am sitting comfortably in California on a salary which was vast in UK terms and the English church is so far behind something needs to be done. I felt like a traitor ignoring all this, so in 1986 I came back across the Atlantic to become a part-time curate at Oxford's Cuddesdon village and chaplain to the theological college – working also for the Ordination of Women to Priesthood movement.

'Because I had been ordained in America they tried to get a licence for me from the archbishop. They were told, "People aren't ready for such a step. The laity won't accept it." Bishop John Yates of Gloucester heard of this and I was licensed as deacon in 1988. I worked as curate at Coleford's St John's for four years and had a marvellous time with the Foresters. I applied for St Briavels mainly to make a point. I didn't think I had a chance but they appointed me anyway, so I became the first woman incumbent in the diocese. In 1994 the archbishop issued a licence for me to act as priest but for the formal ceremony I wanted all us women to go together.' In April that year at Gloucester cathedral she and a dozen or so female deaconesses were 'priested', several thereupon taking up posts at churches around the Forest.

Nonconformists had accepted the principle of women clergy many years earlier. In this as in other respects the established church – in the Forest as

Among the first Church of England women priests in 1994, the Revd Pat Pinkerton at St Mary's, St Briavels. In retirement she assists as curate at Coleford's St John's.

elsewhere – was as in earlier centuries responding to the challenge posed by vigorous alternative Protestant denominations. It is a revelation to find that Sister Jan Mullin, incumbent of Brockweir's Moravian church, was not only a woman priest presiding over a congregation recognized by the Church of England but one which pre-dated England's C of E by several decades.

❖ ❖ ❖

Among the earliest to emerge in Britain were the Baptists. (Although a very early Quaker foundation survives in Ross-on-Wye they were sparse in the Forest.)

The Revd John Skinner, vicar of Weston-under-Penyard during the Civil War, was one of two thousand 'non-juring' clerics who preferred to give up their livings when, under the Restoration, Charles II reintroduced old rituals and doctrinal orthodoxies. Instead he walked fortnightly Sundays to preach to a gathering of Coleford adherents and baptize new converts in the Cannop Brook. The first Newland Street church was built in 1805, the present handsome building replacing it in 1858. Its pastor William Bradley was energetic in taking the message to what were then extremely primitive surrounding hamlets. He was remembered as 'carrying a bible under his arm and a three-legged stool in his hand to stand upon while he proclaimed salvation to the benighted colliers and miners, who at that time were mostly disorderly and ignorant. Often they threw dead cats at him and pelted him with filth, rotten eggs and stones, but he won many to the truth.'

At Aylburton in 1806 Dr Godwin describes how he attempted 'an evangelic experiment among the population then extremely ignorant of the Gospel and deeply prejudiced against all serious religion. I was subjected to an almost incessant form of persecution. I was pelted with stones and rotten eggs. Sparrows were put in through the windows. One night an owl was brought to fight with a cat and on another occasion a tall fellow presented himself with one half of his face blackened and the other part white, having a wig with the hind part before.

'The place where we worshipped was broken into at night and the benches destroyed. These things having been replaced and the windows and doors securely fastened, an opening was soon effected in the wall and in the morning the benches and pulpit were found split to pieces, and even the books torn to fragments. One evening a band of music was heard under our window making the utmost possible discord. Our third set of benches were destroyed before they left the maker's shop and finally the place was again forcibly entered at night, the floor, walls and ceiling covered with disgusting filth, and the door fastened up.' He and colleagues persevered nevertheless, though the Lydney church was not built till 1837. A recent longtime pastor was Eric Chilvers, the church being served after his death in 1994 by lay pastors such as Bill Townsend of Tutnalls Street, in that year president of the Gloucestershire Baptist Association.

At Cinderford, already becoming the Forest's largest town, the original chapel was replaced in 1860 by the imposing church seating 600 worshippers, with spacious Sunday school premises beneath. By 1875 it was already too small and galleries were added to the gigantic building which still dominates the valley. Lacking a pastor in 1996 it was being served as moderator by Pansy Williams from Ross for Sunday services and weekday bible classes. The Ruardean Hill chapel was founded in 1864 by Joseph Mountjoy, the later preaching of the Revd David John Hiley attracting large congregations. The Baptists' eight surviving churches and two chapels include beautiful but remote buildings such as that at Green Bottom on the Littledean to Flaxley Road. When asked who ever went there to worship a neighbour responded, 'You should see it on Christmas Eve. There are so many cars you can't park for a mile around.'

When John Wesley preached at St Briavels in 1749 the locals threw stones. The Revd Derek Balsdon (thirty) encountered a better reception at Cinderford where he arrived in 1993 as probationary minister. A farmer's son from Cornwall, he went to a Derbyshire bible college at twenty-one. As a lay worker assisting a Harrogate minister he met his future wife Hilary, who has since become a lay preacher. After three years at Birmingham's Queen's College with its ecumenical intake he came to Cinderford, and was ordained in 1995. From his modern manse on Cinderford's Somerset Road he ministers not only to the great Wesley church on Belle Vue Road and the Church Road chapel built by the Primitive Methodists in 1866, but to those at Pillowell, Drybrook and Bailey Lane End. 'It is difficult to cover,' he agrees, 'because the same area is ministered to by several Anglican vicars and non-stipendaries.' On Sundays he takes the service at two of the

Cinderford's Methodist minister, the Revd Derek Balsdon, in front of Church Road's Primitive Methodist chapel.

churches. The others are served by retired, visiting or student clergy, or lay preachers. 'My job is discovering where the churches are at and where they need to be heading. With God's help I seek to lead them onwards.'

'Some congregations are falling, some rising,' said the Superintendent of the Forest's Methodist circuit, the Revd John Flintham. From his (modern, of course) manse off Coleford's Cinder Hill he is minister of the chapels at Coalway, Mile End, Bream, Edge End, Ellwood, Clements End, Whitecroft and Woolaston (Lydney's Springfield church and that at Aylburton being served by a minister visiting from Gloucester). 'The Forest proper has never been through the squire-and-parson experience so the free churches get a lot of support. We are in good heart and all the churches cooperate a lot. Baptists, Anglicans and Methodists do all sorts of things together.'

❖ ❖ ❖

The schoolroom of Littledean's United Reformed church was humming on its Wednesday coffee morning. A couple of dozen parishioners were getting ready to tuck into plates of biscuits but beneath the chatter was some sadness. The two ministers, the Revds Andrew and Sally Willett, were leaving the next day after five years in residence. Formed in 1972 from a merger of Presbyterians and Congregationalists, the United Reformed's four existing Forest churches were former Congregational chapels.

The congregation first formed at Newnham where in 1797 the Society of Mission began prayer meetings. 'The house in which the Independents had

Reverends Andrew and Sally Willett at their farewell to Littledean's United Reformed Church.

planned to hold services was broken into, the forms and pulpit stolen, broken and thrown into the river. The windows of the dwelling-place were demolished,' writes former Gloucestershire County Council chairman Eric Radley in his church history. The missioners tried again on Littledean Hill, also location of Cinderford's first Methodist chapel. In 1821 the Congregationalists opened the simple but elegant Broad Street premises, enlarged in 1847 and with the schoolroom added in 1885. Pastor from 1932 to 1946 was the Revd Hezekiah Williams, a Welshman of whom Radley writes, 'He preached with conviction and a rare eloquence, sometimes being carried away almost into incoherence by the ardour with which he proclaimed his message'.

First woman minister was the Revd Phyllis (Paddy) Tee (1976–82). Sally was jointly ordained and inducted with John at St Ethelbert's parish church in 1989, the chapel not being large enough to accommodate a congregation including Catholic and Methodist ministers as well as the Bishop of Tewkesbury. The Willetts were moving on in the Free Church tradition of revolving ministers after a few years. A farewell photograph was needed but it was pouring with rain and the flock were reluctant to leave the schoolroom's shelter. With the pastoral skills gained in his first ministry Andrew sorts things out. 'No biscuits until the photo has been taken,' he shouts, and there is a stampede to the door.

CHAPTER 8

Music

'We have twenty-five youngsters in our junior section but natural wastage means that only three or four usually go on to join the full band,' says Des Yeates (sixty-four), Lydney's Lydmet Band's euphonium player and photographer. 'Youngsters in primary school may be encouraged to take an interest in music but as teenagers they discover other attractions. Society is also changing so much that in the Forest villages and towns the sense of identity with the old mining or manufacturing communities is disappearing.' Born in Lydney, Des played with the Lydbrook and Cinderford bands before returning to Lydney, which six years ago celebrated its hundredth anniversary.

'It was the Great Exhibition of 1851 that saw the beginnings of working class involvement in music. The bands started out as drum and fife bands, fifes being a simple and cheap flute which poor people could afford to buy. They accompanied people in their marches to chapel and on wake days. They evolved into bands with full brass instrumentation later in the nineteenth century, Stalybridge in 1870 being the earliest. Tom Beavan, pastor of the Springfield chapel, inaugurated the Lydney band in 1882. Initially equipped with drums and fifes it became a full brass band in 1892.'

Its chairman Brian White is among its longest-serving musicians. His father was musical director of the Berry Hill band and his own children continue the family tradition. Son Andrew studied music and became a music teacher. Son Kevin started playing at nine and is currently the band's musical director. Practice nights are Monday and Friday evenings at the old gas works site bandroom. Public performances are at ten or so fêtes in summer, Christmas-time visits to hospitals and old folks homes, plus four competitions each year. Early in the year is the annual Stroud contest, area divisional finals are at Bristol in March or April, the Gloucestershire Trophy is at the Royal Forest of Dean College in November.

The Lydney band is in the first section, one down from the championship section and with three below it. 'The top bands in the championship section are semi-professional. Bands such as Sun Life or Black Dyke perform at concerts worldwide, make records, broadcast on radio and TV and receive substantial sponsorship. From this they are able to pay for their instruments, their key players, their premises and other expenses such as musical commissions. Lydmet has sponsored Lydney since 1987 but despite our own fund-raising we have to pass the begging bowl around at Christmas to cover a £16,000 or so deficit.'

Lydney Lydbrook Brass Band.

Each band tends to have an across-the-board mixture of age and talents, a third generally being female. 'Some of us are better than others but as a team we are good. That is the joy of it. There is also a great variety of music in the repertoire, from competition pieces to arrangements of popular pieces. Over the past thirty years, with the vast improvements in the design of instruments, and the degree of dedication of the musicians, standards have improved dramatically. Also, although bands retain a cloth-cap image, they nowadays have a wide range of membership.'

Des, a retired engineering lecturer at a Bristol college, was formerly a member of the Forest of Dean Young People's Band founded by Cecil Chappell (seventy-seven) in 1963. One of the great figures of the band world, Cecil joined the Cinderford band in 1930 as a cornet player. His brother Les, who played drums, also started a dance band. 'For a couple of decades our little sextet played not only in local halls but in places such as Bath, Oxford and the Empress Ballroom in Blackpool,' he reminisces. 'I remember VE night in Lydney town hall in 1945. There were a thousand people there. After midnight the organizer, Mr Hughes, came up to us every hour and offered us an extra fee to carry on – so we played till the small hours.'

Cecil became the Cinderford band's conductor in 1948 at what was then the young age of only twenty-eight. 'It was at a low ebb in those postwar years, having lost a lot of our best players. We started in the fourth section and within six years we were in the championship section.

'In 1972, that never to be forgotten year, we were in the National Championships at the Albert Hall. In 1986 we attracted sponsorship from the late Mr Billy Thomas, who played in the Pillowell band and had a music business and dance band in Gloucester. He expanded his interests in all directions, including property and the Swanbrook coach company, so we became the Cinderford

Swanbrook Band – and Billy's grandson Keith continues to be very good to us.'

Of the Youth Band, Des recalls that 'Cecil trained a lot of youngsters at the schools, even if they didn't go on to join the band. Some years you can teach hundreds of children and only get one good enough to play in competition. Other years it might be ten.' The band started foreign tours, making a dozen trips to Holland and Germany. Des remembers that while on the coach (driver Harry Grindle) Cecil used to point out all the sights and explain their history. 'One time at a spa town he insisted we all drank from the medicinal springs. The water was full of Epsom salts and within minutes Cecil was telling everyone to look out for a public lavatory – urgently.'

Cecil's memories of changes since that time include the increase in the number of women players. 'In the old

Cecil Chappell.

days, even in the 1950s, it was very uncommon to have a woman in the band – we were one of the first. Now we have six girls out of the twenty-four main players. In fact the girls are more interested than the boys. The young people are more intelligent as regards music. It is a pleasure working with them, because the standards of playing used to leave a lot to be desired.'

At the 1998 Stroud annual competition for Gloucestershire's brass bands Forest bands in the first section came first, second and third: Lydbrook, Lydney and Forest Brass. Chairman of the Gloucestershire Brass Band Association, which today numbers thirty-nine bands, is Lydbrook's Robert Morgan – another major figure in recent Forest band history, together with the band's conductor Brian Howard. He joined in 1955 as a cornet player, with a musical background stretching back to the beginning of the century when the family formed its own band.

'The Morgan family consisted of eight sons and three daughters, every one of whom could play an instrument. The bandmaster was Augustus Morgan who was killed at Trafalgar Colliery in 1912,' writes Maurice Bent in his *The Musical Tradition of the Forest* (1997) – Robert being Augustus's grandson. During the 1960s the band suffered as a consequence of its own success, many of its best players leaving for championship section bands. 'Robert Morgan was elected musical director in 1969 [having] done much to revive the band, to train new

Robert Morgan (centre back) with Lydbrook band's musical director Brian Howard (third from left) and (to his left) star soloist Brett Baker.

players, turning the tide and going in for competitions.' While continuing as a player, he handed over the conductor's baton in 1980 to Berry Hill-born Lyndon Baglin, for years the country's top euphonium player.

'He told us he was going to take us to the championship section,' says Robert. 'We all had a good laugh about that.' In 1987 they were there, Lyndon retiring on his laurels the next year. Conductor since 1991 has been Brian Howard, another star of the national scene having been resident conductor of Bristol's Sun Life. Moving to the Forest he was first with the Yorkley Onward Band, which in 1995 merged with the Coleford band to form Forest Brass. He took the Lydbrook band to the national championships at the Wembley Conference Centre in 1994 and now presides over a lively bandroom with enough young players having joined to form a junior training band. The band and Lydbrook school collaborate in a scheme whereby a music teacher visits the school once a week. 'The youngsters need encouragement or the musical traditions will die out,' he says.

❖ ❖ ❖

The sound of music echoes as loudly in Bream as in Lydbrook, the village having its own notable band and one-time male voice choir. One of the band's cornet players was Robert Walkerdine who in the 1980s joined with a group of former Bream choir singers to form the Forest of Dean Male Voice Choir with Robert as musical director from 1986. Accompanist Yvonne Andrews became assistant

Musical director Robert Walkerdine in 1993 at the centre (front row) of the Royal Forest of Dean Male Voice Choir.

musical director in 1991 and was succeeded by Kate Nelmes, then a pupil at Whitecross school. As well as being a piano player Kate was principal horn for Pillowell's Silver Band at the age of fifteen, member of the National Youth Brass Band of Great Britain, horn soloist at the choir's public concerts, and is now an expert commentator on the Forest's musical scene. Also called on for concert solos was Tracey Screen, Robert's younger sister, and principal cornet with the Bream Silver Band.

The choir is forty strong. 'Any less and you have not got the volume,' says committee member Brian James. 'Any more and it becomes difficult to manage.' Their repertoire is impressively varied. A typical programme might kick off with the romantic Cornish folk song 'White Rose' followed by a bouncy Italian number. 'Nothing Like A Dame' from *South Pacific* leads into the hymn 'Deus Salutis'. Other renditions are followed by an entracte of voice or brass solos. The second half may kick off with 'Forest Gold' succeeded by up-tempo 'When The Saints Come Marching In'. Lloyd Webber's 'Love Changes Everything' is a popular standard, a climax being provided by the 'Chant' from Dylan Thomas's *Under Milkwood*.

Voice soloists include Marina Lambert, also of Bream, who is renowned for recitals of her poems and anecdotes, usually in Forest dialect. On a previous year's

Drybrook and District Male Voice Choir at their one-time telephone exchange rehearsal room.

tour to Cornwall the soloist had been Becky Morgan, later becoming the choir's musical director. At Lydney's 1998 Poppy Appeal concert performed by the choir and Lydmet Band, Becky's thirteen-year-old son played percussion in the band for the first time.

❖ ❖ ❖

'There has been a great tradition of choral singing in the Forest since the turn of the century, but the old habits of singing in church have almost died out,' says Hubert Evans (seventy-three), member of the Drybrook and District Male Voice Choir almost from its creation in 1948. His wife Winifred had served as accompanist since 1952. Both are from Lydbrook, where Hubert was once the barber, and later at Cinderford, before working at Rank Xerox until his retirement. Increasing age is no bar to continuing participation, he says. 'We can project more volume than ever. But the older you get the more you need to keep in trim, so with my wife's help on the piano I practice my scales every day.'

Long-time music director was June Jones, wife of choir secretary Malcolm Jones. Organist at Drybrook church, she is an accomplished mezzo-soprano and concert soloist. Her own music teacher, Margaret Thomas, Professor of Music at Birmingham University, was a soloist for the choir for many years, and is now its president. 'The two of them have brought new techniques to the choir,' says Hubert, whose own daughter became a music teacher. 'We have so much to offer young people but you have to capture them first. Unless we make a link between the generations we will go down.' The choir's theme song is, appropriately, 'Take Me Home'. 'It relates to the old Forest, the song of the miners returning from the pit singing, "That's one more day, we're glad to see the sunshine".'

❖ ❖ ❖

The full story of the Forest's bands is told by Maurice Bent (sixty-four) in *The Musical Traditions of the Forest* mentioned above. In a later volume he will be covering the choirs, including the Springfield ladies choir and smaller female choral groups such as the Sylvan Singers. He was born in the Ruardean cottage now occupied by his daughter. An old photograph shows his grandfather and extensive family outside the cottage with his donkey and trap. 'He ran trips with the cart down to Cinderford and back on Saturday nights,' says Maurice.

Having previously worked as a coffin maker Maurice then worked as a carpenter at the Northern United colliery for sixteen years until its closure in

1965. He became an organ builder, then moved to Rank's until ill health pushed him back into self-employment as an organ builder once again, in partnership with Keith Jones of The Pludds. Organist at the Baptist church on Ruardean Hill, where he and his wife Doreen live, he shows off the organ's array of blue painted pipes and the workings behind. Bought secondhand from Huddersfield in 1906, it turned out to be one of the finest pipe organs in Britain. When rebuilding it to face the congregation in 1983, he found a card inside which suggests it was built, or given an early overhaul, by Gray and Davidson in as early as 1790.

As he demonstrates its purity of tone, the noise rippling round the chapel's lean walls, he talks of the Royal Forest of Dean Organ Society founded by the previous minister in 1967 – Maurice is still its secretary. As well as attending recitals at churches and chapels around the Forest its members visit further afield. The previous year Maurice and

The Forest's musical historian Maurice Bent at the Ruardean Hill Baptist Church organ he has played and repaired since the 1960s.

others had been given the opportunity to play the organ of Westminster Abbey. Connoisseurs from elsewhere return the visits and there are occasional concerts in the chapel – such as that held a few years ago (soloist June Jones) to celebrate the centenary of Lydney born composer Herbert Howells. 'We have also had oratorios here, though it's a bit of squash for a full choir, orchestra and soloists.'

Having collected reminiscences from older inhabitants of Ruardean Hill he wrote and published *Highest Point of Dean* (1985), generously illustrated with old photographs. He followed this up with *The Last Deep Mine of Dean* based on memories of former Northern United colleagues. Most recently he produced the first part of his musical history having accumulated material for years. On the table of his bungalow opposite the former Nag's Head sits the Demonstration Challenge Cup won in 1939 by the Ruardean band. Maurice has managed to track this and others down, several now forming a display of Forest eisteddfod cups at the Dean Heritage Centre. The contests alternated between Lydney town hall and the Ruardean Baptist church but stopped during the last war. The traditional Ruardean band contest ended in 1978. 'I looked up old records and traced people who had connections with the old bands and choirs. They looked in their cupboards and attics and were sometimes surprised by what they found.'

The most extraordinary collection of musical instruments is to be found at Drybrook in the former grounds of the Euroclydon mansion. Coalmaster William Brain built the house with a tower tall enough for him to be able to climb up each morning to see if the engine house chimney of his Trafalgar colliery over the hill was smoking satisfactorily, or whether his men had taken an impromptu 'holiday'. It later became a hotel and was bought in 1971 by Stan Brown. After his death it was sold and became a home for the elderly. Stan and his wife had built themselves a modern bungalow next door, which passed to their daughter Gill and her husband Wally Marfell. They also inherited the results of Stan's collecting passion.

In 1950 he had bought a 1900 polyphon for a fiver. 'No one wanted such things after the war,' says Gill. His interest in mechanical music machines took hold and he acquired so many he had to build a small hangar to house them. When Wally took early retirement as manager of MEB's Ross-on-Wye office seven years ago he had more time to look after the collection. They had tried to give the lot to a local museum but the curators took the view that the instruments needed specialist care which they couldn't guarantee. 'We didn't want to sell them but at the same time it was sad no one was able to enjoy them. So last year [1994] we put them on show for a cancer charity.'

Wally Marfell in the musical museum he and his wife Gill have assembled from her father's collection at Drybrook's Euroclydon mansion.

Since then they have opened their Dean Organ Museum through the summer, the proceeds again going to charity. They are one of the fifty or so UK museums listed in the Fair Organs Preservation Society handbook and have used their holidays to visit others in France and elsewhere on the Continent. Entering the hangar you find yourself on what might be the set for a magical pantomime. There are dozens of small musical contraptions, such as a musical-box hidden in a mock book, ancient radios and a couple of ornate accordions which Gill and Wally used to play.

The strangest looking machines are the polyphons which have huge metal discs operating the musical works concealed in their gleaming wood cabinets. Even earlier is an enormous Imhof and Muckle barrel orchestrion, operated by great metal-toothed cylinders controlling the flow of air to its pipes. The Germans Imhof and Muckle worked in England from 1850 to 1874, thus dating the orchestrion to that period. Wally switches it on and it plays with total perfection of sound. He then disappears behind the garish 1930s 'Arburo', the café dance organ operated by a strip of printed card which was a predecessor of the jukebox. It blasts into life, lights flashing and the instruments – accordion, wooden castanets and saxophone – playing as though fingered by invisible hands.

They hadn't yet got around to cataloguing the whole collection and were having difficulty in finding experts able to restore the machines. Outside Wally points to a vintage car that is the product of his own collecting. Gill adds, 'Our son collects vintage tractors, if you would like to have a look at them . . .'.

Gill Marfell and another example from the Dean Organ Museum, the Imhof and Muckle barrel orchestrion.

CHAPTER 9

Writers

'They rag me about it at school,' wails Bernard Kear (sixty-one) of his Drybrook primary school pupils' reaction to the publication of his *Scenes of Childhood*. Its seventy or so drawings depict Forest cottagers' life of the late 1930s and early 1940s. His childhood was twenty years after the decades of dreadful poverty vividly described by Winifred Foley (now eighty-four) in her *A Child of the Forest*, but most Forest families suffered daily hardship which was, paradoxically, only eased when the war boosted employment in the mines and other industries. When his brother came back from New Zealand for a holiday Bernard's sketches were shown around like family snapshots. 'My nephews and nieces couldn't understand what seemed so primitive to them. Since publication a lot of people have said, "Gosh you were poor!"

'It is true we didn't have a lot of money but we had the right things. Kids today are a lot poorer. They are suffering from the effects of divorces or unemployment, stresses which are much different than in our time. They have television and crisps every day but they don't get taken for walks. We were very wealthy in the things that mattered.'

The youngest boy among eight brothers and sisters, Bernard was eight by the end of the war. Their mother had died young and the kids were brought up at their Oldcroft cottage by their father, who started life as a carpenter, until a housekeeper arrived a year later. 'Dad was a fitter who worked at the Whitecroft pin factory. It was our oldest brother Den and sister Cynthia who became father and mother to us. They used to patch our clothes, mend our shoes, generally look after us. I am still a little scared of "our Den".'

Brother Alec still lives in the cottage, now modernized. Eldest brother Dennis is retired, as are the two other brothers, now living in Devon and New Zealand. Of his two surviving sisters, one still lives in the Forest and the other in Yorkshire. Bernard followed in his brothers' footsteps to Lydney grammar school. 'Our Dad was pleased we went there but didn't believe in things like homework. When we got home there were jobs to be done like the gardening. So I had to do my homework in playtime, or on the school bus back, or during other classes.'

Dennis went to work at the Whitecroft pin factory. Bernard, who had enjoyed fiddling around with radios, became an electrician. Having married and had children, he began studying by correspondence course. 'Thank God for technical colleges. The principals of the Gloucester and Cinderford colleges were marvellous. Once I had two exams on the same day and they arranged a car to get

*Youngest boy among eight brothers and sisters, retired Drybrook schoolteacher
Bernard Kear has produced two books of sketches of their Oldcroft cottage upbringing.*

*Bernard Kear with his brothers and sister. Back, left to right: Gerald and Dennis;
front: Alec, Olive and Bernard himself.*

me from one to the other.' Qualifying at teacher training college, he went to Drybrook School from which he retired a couple of years ago.

He started drawing as a child. 'We all enjoyed drawing but had hardly any paper. The margins of the newspaper were useful to work on, and the occasional used envelope was a coveted prize. I took up painting and wildlife sculptures years later. I think it was a hangover from childhood days when Dad would say, "If you haven't anything to do I'll find something for thee".'

The book's sections follow the year from the spring planting of 'Taters and greens' through the arduous daily task of collecting 'Water for drinking and washing' to descriptions of sabbaths and holidays. Sundays meant tedious visits to chapel. Saturdays were more enjoyable, allowing walks to the Blackpool brook where they launched boats and built mud dams. 'But our Dad would expect each of us to be carrying an armload of firewood to toss on the woodpile on the way back.'

A special treat was going to the rocks beneath the Purton railway bridge. 'To us it was one of the wonders of the world. The size of it, with the trains roaring across, seemed magnificent.The only trouble was the walk back home uphill.' During their walks their father taught them about the world around them. 'Children today know very little about the natural world. Our dad could name most of the flowers we saw. On Boxing Day we used to visit our grandparents. On the way back it was very quiet – no traffic, no planes in the sky. Dad would stop and show us the stars, the Pleiades, the Great Bear and Orion and his belt. Afterwards we would scramble around in the undergrowth and come home with a bundle of firewood.'

Of his career at the school Bernard said, 'A job is as good as the people you work with and they have been wonderful. The children too are so nice. You are compelled to do your darndest for them. I've enjoyed it all thoroughly.' He was apprehensive, though, about the imminent publication of a second volume. It covers episodes through the year such as the raising and autumn slaughter of the family pig. 'I'll get ragged about it again at school,' he says mournfully. He adds that he can't really claim to be a writer, rather an illustrator, yet his extended captions capture Forest dialect exactly.

❖ ❖ ❖

An even harder childhood was narrated by Joyce Latham in *Where I Belong*. Born in the workhouse, which could have provided an alternative title for her memoirs, she was the illegitimate child of a servant girl by the son of the grand house where her mother was in service. She was about to be fostered out by the parish when her grandmother intervened and thereafter brought her up as her own child at her and her husband's Hillersland home. Her natural mother later married and brought up five children. 'We led our separate lives but remained friendly,' says Joyce.

From Christchurch school she gained one of the two annual scholarships to the Bells grammar school. 'They gave me £3 to cover everything for the year, so during the war I went blackberrying to earn my pocket money – selling the fruit to the Rising Sun at Five Acres.' After school she worked in a paper shop, then for the grocer's William and Cotton, then at Lydney's Pine End factory. She

Joyce Latham, author of A Forest of Dean Childhood in the 1930s, *with late husband Bob in front of the Christchurch schoolroom.*

met her husband Bob at a dance where he was playing drums. 'I liked the look of him though he appeared a bit miserable, so I got stuck with him for forty years.'

In Coleford's Feathers Hotel, the previous venue for the Forest Folk Club which the pair participated in, Bob tries to retaliate. 'I could tell some things about her . . .' – but he is silenced by Joyce's command. 'You keep your mouth shut. Don't spoil my image.' Their home (although Bob died last year) was on Coleford's Sunny Bank estate with their daughter living nearby. One of their two sons, a graphic designer working at Sutton Publishing, illustrated her book.

Like Winifred Foley she started scribbling and reciting poetry from a young age. 'A friend recently recited one of my early poems word for word, which was amazing since she heard it when she was seven or eight.' Having shoved a wad of poems through Doug McLean's letterbox and got them printed, she became much in demand as a performer. 'I go all over the Forest – to churches, community centres, old folks homes – anyone who can't run away.' Some of her poems are in standard English, others in Forest dialect. Among the former, 'Starting School' has become a GCSE exam set text. 'I had the same teacher as Dennis Potter four years later. He was very supportive. But Bob is nowadays my best critic, which is what Winnie [Foley] says about her Syd.' 'But you can't stand criticism,' says Bob rebelliously. Pretending not to hear him she says, 'Scratch any Forester and he or she has a story to tell.'

Blaisdon farmer Humphrey Phelps, author of fictionalized memoirs of rural life before, during and after the war, with wife Pauline at Boseley Court Farm.

At the entrance to Boseley Court Farm, in the parish of Westbury, there is a sign with the head of a Red Poll bull, 'When we came here in 1953,' said Humphrey Phelps, 'we started keeping Red Poll cattle and they've been keeping us ever since. They are dual purpose – that is, they produce milk and beef. Of course they're very unfashionable, there are hardly any herds left in the country now. But then, we're unfashionable and I don't suppose there are many farmers like us left today,'

He lights his pipe and starts to talk about farming, life, literature and politics. His grandfather and father were farmers, his grandfather had a farm at Mitcheldean, much of it now covered by the Rank factory and houses.

When he was eleven, Humphrey went to the Crypt Grammar School in Gloucester. 'I managed to evade most attempts to educate me, I'm rather pleased about that. But Mr Hook, who taught English, gave me a love of words and reading, I'm even more pleased about that. Although I dare say I'd have been a more successful farmer if I hadn't been so fond of books.'

While at Crypt he briefly met the girl who became his wife in 1951, she being at Ribston Hall School, close to where Crypt boys played cricket. 'I remember it well.' 'No you don't,' says Pauline, his wife.

His first published articles appeared in the left-wing weekly *Tribune* in the early 1970s. Since then he's written for several magazines and for almost twenty years regularly for *The Countryman*. His first book, *Just Around the Corner* (Thornhill Press, 1974, Alan Sutton paperback, 1987), was written in about three weeks. 'It's fiction, you can tell more of the truth in fiction, and the story is told through the eyes of a child', he says of it.

The next book took six months, in between working on the farm. Called *Just Across the Fields* (1976), it was published by Michael Joseph and Sphere paperback in 1978. 'It had a lot of good reviews, forty or more, I think. It didn't make me rich or famous, but the Royal Society of Literature did make me a Fellow.' *Just Over Yonder* (1977) and *Just Where We Belong* (1978), both published by Michael Joseph, completed his farming trilogy.

'A few years later Alan Sutton wrote and asked me to write a whole book about Uncle George, the hard-drinking rascal who'd featured in my previous books, and a book about the Forest of Dean. While writing *The Forest of Dean* (1982), I realised I was in love with the Forest. The first print sold out in less than a week and was hastily reprinted. Since then it's been reprinted several times and is still in print. At the launch of *The Forest of Dean in Old Photographs* (1983), Alan Sutton told me to go home and write the Uncle George book. *Uncle George and Company* was published the following year (paperback, 1987) and so was another collection of old photographs of the Forest.'

Other books followed. *Country Anecdotes* (Robert Hale, 1990), *Southwold to Aldeburgh* (Sutton, 1991), *Around Woodbridge* (Sutton, 1992), *Suffolk A Hundred Years Ago* (Sutton, 1992), *A Suffolk Christmas* (Sutton, 1991), *The Heart of Suffolk* (Sutton, 1993), *A Forest Christmas* (Sutton, 1993), *An Essex Christmas* (Sutton, 1993), *From Forest to Severn* (Chalford Press, 1994), *Lowestoft to Southwold* (Chalford Press, 1994), *Walberswick to Felixstowe* (Chalford Press, 1994), *The Forest of Dean in Wartime* (Sutton, 1995) and *Forest Voices* (Chalford Press, 1996).

Perhaps unusually for a farmer, he was also active in the Labour Party, and was Chairman of the West Gloucestershire party in the 1970s. Since then he's not been involved. He's now turned seventy, still farms, grows all his own vegetables, writes articles – but only against a deadline – and might write another book.

On a muddy Hewelsfield lane in midwinter, crime writer Andrew Taylor (forty-seven) and retired forester Bart Venner stand below a tree where, in Andrew's latest book, a body is found hanging. The first of what was intended as a trilogy of detective stories set in 'Lydmouth', an old market town on the England–Wales border in the late 1940s and early 1950s, *An Air That Kills* (1993) had introduced a cast of characters making up a small town society. 'It is like *Middlemarch* but with bodies,' Andrew says with relish, having become (Winifred Foley apart) the Forest's bestselling author.

Having settled in Coleford with his wife Caroline sixteen years ago, he borrows local names which it is fun spotting. For historical research he reads back numbers of local papers, including *The Forester* at its Cinderford office. 'It was absolutely fascinating. Life was much more stable in some ways, full of uncertainty in others. You find stories such as "Driver crashes into sheep – no one injured". People were frequently being injured in the mines but this was deemed to be less newsworthy for some reason.'

Best-selling crime writer Andrew Taylor at Newland's All Saints parish church, centrepiece of one of his 'Lydmouth' mysteries.

Some of the origins for his fictional locations are recognizable. Characters pop in and out of Lydmouth's old Bull Hotel, similar to the Angel Hotel with its rear courtyard and stables. In the second book, *The Mortal Sickness* (1995), a body is found in the chapel of the parish church. 'I took the church at Newland very much as my model, though of course the vicar and his wife in my story are wholly imaginary. Newland has a very mysterious quality. Its churchyard dominates the village, with the main buildings lying around it. The sense of its past oozes out of the almshouses and former grammar school.'

Son of an East Anglian clergyman, Andrew began writing while working as a London librarian. His early books such as *Caroline Minuscule* (1982) featured the unusual amateur detective William Dougal, who was not above committing a murder or two himself if circumstances required. Eighth and latest in the series was *Odd Man Out* (1994) in which there is scarcely a single sympathetic character. 'I like my nasty characters,' Andrew admits cheerfully. There were also thrillers such as *The Second Midnight* (1988), *Blacklist* (1988) and *Toyshop* (1990), as well the psychological thrillers *The Raven on the Water* (1991) and *The Barred Window* (1993). Latest in the series is the Roth Trilogy, beginning with *The Four Last Things* (1997) in which the protagonist is a female paedophile murderer. Demonstrating that a writer's life is less easy than it seems, Andrew has also written under a pen name half a dozen thrillers for teenagers, ghosted several stories linked to TV series, contributed short stories to women's magazines, and does a regular stint as publisher's reader.

The idea for *The Lover of the Grave* (1997), with its more rural backdrop, came from a family walk along the green way which was formerly the main route between Hewelsfield and St Briavels. 'Even on a summer's day the setting had a very strong atmosphere,' Andrew says. Some of the key characters live in the remote farmsteads alongside it, while the local village bobby and others meet in 'Ashbridge's' Beaufort Arms. In St Briavels' George Hotel, the real-life Beaufort Arms, Bart Venner is able to tell Andrew of a real body found near the Hewelsfield crossroads. The Carpenters Arms pub stood here before road widening and one evening one of the regulars set off home at closing time but never arrived. 'His body was found the next morning. His head had been struck by a metal object. He could have struck his head on an iron gate or someone may have hit him. To complicate things he probably didn't die where he was found, so somebody may have moved him.'

Bart moved here thirty years ago when working for the Forestry Commission, having been on the same course at Parkend training school as John Everard. It was livelier in those days, he remembers. 'When half the Forest was on the dole, it was quite a sight on Thursdays outside the pubs when people got their benefit.' The police section house closed down only fairly recently, the last bobby having been a woman. Andrew has his notebook out and scribbles away, for the Lydmouth books have been so well received his publishers have commissioned a further three, the most recently published being *The Suffocating Night* (1998). So a lot more bodies? 'I can guarantee that,' Andrew nods. 'Which means making a few adjustments to history. I checked the records for the county in the decade after the Second World War and the average was one murder per year. That would never do.'

CHAPTER 10

Historians

The prospect from the bay window of Parkend's Fountain Inn is of a peaceful scene, sheep browsing along the roadside, pretty cottages, a tall stone building housing a field studies centre, and a few passing cars. It is difficult to imagine that a hundred and fifty years ago this was a frenetic, smoky and noisy landscape teeming with people and machines. Wagons came jolting down the railways from coal and iron mines up the Cannop and Oakwood valleys. Smoke belched from the tall engine house of the ironworks and furnace behind it, while the din from hammering rose above everything. 'There is probably more history in Parkend than in any other Forest village,' says Ralph Anstis (seventy-seven) who came here with his wife Bess, also a retired civil servant, twenty years ago.

To occupy his retirement he researched the past of his adopted village and wrote the booklet *Parkend, The Story of a Dean Forest Village* (1982). Contributing occasional articles on Forest places and people to *The Forester*, he had them published in a booklet *Around the Forest*. It included a gripping piece of detective work among public records which showed how the Deputy Surveyor Edward Machen was hounded out of office but then exonerated and begged to return until a successor had been found. Since then there have been three major biographies of Forest individuals and families, a collection of mini-biographies and a book of short stories.

The couple moved in 1984 to Coalway's Albion House, the former Albion Inn. 'Like most Forest pubs it was the meeting place for working class people,' says Ralph. 'They held miners meetings here – the miners' leader Timothy Mountjoy, spoke here in 1874 – until it was closed down in 1912 because of suspicions of immorality. I can't see how this was possible, because the upstairs room was wall to wall with a fireplace at each end, a meeting room rather than a bedroom.' He became interested in how Foresters reacted to the enclosure of woodlands early in the nineteenth century and in particular the story of Warren James. In *Warren James and the Dean Forest Riots* (1986), immaculately published under his own Albion House imprint, he recounted how James became involved in the 1831 disturbances which so alarmed local magistrates that they called in troops. 'It wasn't a real riot. There was no damage to property and no one was hurt. All they did was to knock down the barriers erected by the Office of Woods to keep their animals out of the woods. But the authorities decided to make an example of him.'

Anstis then switched his attention to Coleford's early industrialists with *The Industrial Teagues and the Forest of Dean* (1990). 'The Teagues were on the other

'Honorary Forester' Ralph Anstis, biographer of Warren James, the Teagues and the Mushets, in front of Parkend's old ironworks engine house.

side of the fence from Warren James. James Teague was probably a very nasty individual but he was bright and tough and within a couple of generations the family had become gentry. He had a pit north-east of Coleford in the 1790s and introduced a tramway to take the coal to Lydbrook for transportation up the Wye to Ross. His son Moses Teague later tried to introduce steam trains to the Forest but was blocked by other tramway owners. This generation of Teagues were a lively lot but their line doesn't seem to have continued in the Forest. Present-day Teagues come from a different branch of the family.'

When reviewing this book Humphrey Phelps aptly called Anstis 'an honorary Forester'. So immersed had he become in Forest history that the next book was a collection of short stories based on real people. He followed this up by editing, with Bess, the manuscript diary of Bill Williams, a 24-year-old bachelor who worked at the Trafalgar colliery pithead. *The Diary of a Working Man, 1872–3* (1994) is an immensely poignant account of the hard conditions of daily life at the pit and in Bill's Cinderford lodgings. There is no hope of marrying and settling down with his sweetheart Becky, in service in Cheltenham, his income being so inadequate. At the end of the year's diary, a best friend having died, he gives up writing and fades from view.

Four Personalities from the Forest of Dean featured Sir John Winter of Lydney (1602–*c.* 1685), Flaxley Abbey's Catherina Bovey (1670–1726), miners' leader Timothy Mountjoy (1824–96) and Sir Charles Dilke, Forest MP 1892–1911. Sir

John's life reads like a costume movie. From the Whitecross manor inherited from his grandfather, one of Queen Elizabeth's admirals at the Armada, Sir John set about leasing as much of the Forest as possible to supply charcoal for his Lydney ironworks. Also prominent on the national stage, he became private secretary to Charles I's queen Henrietta Maria. As a Catholic, during the Civil War he made Whitecross a bastion against the Parliamentarians based at Gloucester. When Henrietta Maria fled to France he accompanied her in the action-packed escape across the Channel. Returning to take part in the two battles of Beachley, he escaped over what became known as Wintour's Leap. He returned from France after the king's execution but his estate was confiscated and he was imprisoned in the Tower of London for four years. After the Restoration he regained his property and began the building of the first Lydney Park mansion, completed by his son Charles.

Catharina Boevey we will encounter at Flaxley Abbey, and Mountjoy and Dilke at the Speech House. Ralph's latest book is *Man of Iron, Man of Steel* (1997). Recounting the lives of David (1772–1847) and Robert Mushet (1811–91), it tells how the father was a pioneering metallurgist influential in the Forest iron industry's growth in the early nineteenth century. His son, born at Coleford's Tump House, now the Forest House Hotel, spent years experimenting at the Darkhill furnace started by his father. He perfected Sir Henry Bessemer's hitherto imperfect process for making good, cheap steel. Bessemer borrowed the improvement and made a fortune. Robert never became rich, although he also invented a method of making first-class machine tool steel, until recently still known in the USA as 'RMS' – Robert Mushet Steel. Father and son are commemorated by a plaque on the Forest House Hotel installed by the Forest of Dean Local History Society. Why, one wonders, had no one attempted a single volume history of the Forest? 'I would love to have another fifty years of life to do it,' says Ralph, 'but that obviously isn't possible.'

❖ ❖ ❖

Forest historian Dr Cyril Hart has devoted fifty years researching and chronicling most aspects of the Forest's history since his first article 'The Extent and Boundaries of the Forest of Dean and Hundred of St Briavels' was published in 1947. His *The Verderers and Speech-Court of the Forest of Dean* (1950) was quickly followed by *The Commoners of Dean Forest* (1951) and *The Free Miners of the Royal Forest of Dean and Hundred of St Briavels* (1953). Dr Hart has an international reputation in the forestry world. *Taxation of Woodlands*, a standard booklet, has appeared in ten editions, and *Practical Forestry for the Agent and Surveyor*, now in its third edition, was originally published in 1967. His *British Trees in Colour*, written for a more general audience, sold an impressive 60,000 copies in all its editions.

Born in the Forest of Dean and residing in Coleford, Dr Hart studied as a chartered land surveyor and agent, complemented by his earlier MA, MSc (Oxon) and PhD degrees. He became a lecturer in forestry and estate management at Cirencester's Royal Agricultural College. Thereafter he acted as a forestry consultant throughout the UK and chairman of nursery and sawmill companies. From his wide travels as a consultant he produced a report on 'Forestry in Europe' for the Council of Europe in 1979 and a further report for the United Nations

Food and Agriculture Organization the following year. He became a Verderer in 1952, Senior Verderer ten years later, and in 1981 was awarded an OBE for services to forestry. He is an Inclosure Commissioner for the Forest, and is chairman of Forest of Dean Newspapers Ltd.

Dr Hart's books and occasional publications, which are so central to Forest historiography, are comprehensively listed in Further Reading. *Royal Forest: A History of Dean's Woods as producers of Timber* was published by the Oxford University Press in 1966. Dr Hart followed this with *The Industrial History of Dean* (1971), and he put his home town under the historical microscope in *Coleford: The History of a West Gloucestershire Forest Town* (1983). His most recent book is *The Forest of Dean: New History 1550–1818* (1995).

Doyen of Forest historians Dr Cyril Hart in his Coleford garden.

 ❖ ❖ ❖

Single subject histories by a host of local historians are an invaluable record of various aspects of Forest life. In the 1970s the Revd George Lawrence contributed a series of articles to what was then *The Mercury* and is now *The Forester*. As a young Methodist minister he was sent to Lydney's Hill Street chapel in 1927 but after moving away married a Pillowell girl. The couple thereafter worked at churches abroad and latterly in Sussex but frequently revisited the Forest and retired there, George becoming pastor of the Whitecroft church. While his articles centred on Methodist chapels and notable figures, *Kindling of the Flame: 150 Years of Methodism in the Forest of Dean 1824–1974* (1974) provided a rich picture of village life during and before his own acquaintance with the area. George also wrote a history of the Primitive Methodists, *The Bible Christians of the Forest of Dean* (1985) and Tom Bright penned and published *The Rise of Nonconformity in the Forest of Dean* (1954).

R.A.J. Bell, secretary of the Bathursts' Parkend Colliery Company's Norchard colliery, and senior churchwarden of Lydney parish church, added to his history of Lydney hospital his booklet *The Parish Church of St Mary, Lydney* (1983). He bequeathed his large collection of local books to the church. Altruistically, while they could have sold them to contribute towards roof repairs, the parochial church council gave them on permanent loan to Lydney library. An all-too-rare history of a Forest colliery was produced by Dr Graham Field with his *A Look Back at Norchard* (1986), David Bick having written and published *The Old Industries of Dean* in 1979.

Individual town and village histories included John Powell's *A Look at Lydney* with dozens of old photographs; Jack Cockburn's *Staunton* (1996), enterprisingly published by the Friends of All Saints Church; and Margaret Willis's *The Ferry Between Newnham and Arlingham* (1993). As oral history becomes recognized as an important source of history, the typescript 'Memories of Mitcheldean' (1964), collected by students of a Bristol University adult education course, deserves a more permanent form of publication. For local schools, Double View School's history teacher Ray Allen produced in the 1980s a series of town and village histories such as 'The Lydney File' which could also usefully be reprinted.

Following the efforts of the Forest of Dean Newspapers and Doug McLean, a third local publisher arrived when John Pemberthy bought the Thornhill Press and launched a series of local titles from his Parkend base. In its brief life its publications included Bryan Walters' *The Archaeology and History of Ancient Dean and the Wye Valley* (1992) and Mabel Beech's *Wye Valley & Forest of Dean Guide* (1994). Bryan, founder of the Dean Archaeology Group (DAG), suffered a stroke shortly after, which prevented him from completing the Pemberthy-commissioned guide. Mabel, a longtime contributor of historical articles to *The Forester* and active in Drybrook affairs – as a member of Holy Trinity's church council and chairman of the parish council – did the job instead. Similarly active in Cinderford and as a *Forester* contributor was Elsie Olivey, stalwart of institutions such as the town's annual pantomime and the Dean Heritage Centre, where she works weekly as a volunteer archivist.

The Forest of Dean Local History Society unveiling a plaque to the Mushets on their Coleford home. From left, back: Ruth Hirst, Diane Watkins, Harry Daniels, Donald Hicks, Norman Kenneth (Forest House Hotel owner), Dr Cyril Hart, Jim Stewart (district council chief planner), Ian Standing (former Dean Heritage Centre director); front, Maurice Hall, Dr Margaret Barton (Staunton parish council chairman), June Webb, Brian Johns and Keith Webb.

A fourth publisher, and the Forest's third bookshop, appeared when Neil Parkhouse opened the Archive Bookshop opposite the Watts garage in Lydney. As industrial and transport history specialists the shop became part of the national network serving this market of passionate aficionados. As early as 1963 H.W. Paar had published the first of his two-volume history of the Forest's railways, *The Severn & Wye Railway*, following it two years later with *The Great Western Railway in Dean* (1965). Alec Pope's son Ian, having been taken by his father on photographic expeditions around Forest railways as a youngster, embarked on a detailed written and illustrated account of the network with the first volume of *The Severn & Wye Railway* (1983) co-written with Bob How and Paul Karau and published by the latter's Wild Swan press.

After a further two volumes they embarked on *The Forest of Dean Branch*, finishing the job off with a second volume on *The Churchway and Whimsey Branches* (1997). More than just a painstaking history of the railways, the books include text on former railside industries, illustrated with unique photographs from the collections of Alec, Ian, Neil Parkhouse and others. The latter two collaborated in the founding of the Lightmoor Press named after the colliery. It publishes the national industry and transport quarterly magazine *Archive* and the Forest of Dean Local History Society annual journal *The New Regard* and has plans to publish local books such as an expanded new edition of Ralph Anstis' *Parkend*.

❖ ❖ ❖

Press officer for the impressively active Forest of Dean Local History Society is Brian Johns (sixty-five) who, in his Blakeney back garden, demonstrates gifts akin to sorcery. Holding two slim copper rods in his hands he shows a spot where a dig had revealed a circle of potholes from an early hut beside the Bideford brook. As he approaches the rods begin to quiver, eventually crossing over the posthole. Photographer Steve Cassidy remarks he thought dowsing was for divining water. 'If you want water I have to think water,' says Brian. Though his back is to the stream, the loosely held rods swivel 180 degrees to point behind him. This is real magic, though Brian's skill as a dowser has been confirmed a hundredfold by subsequent excavations.

A Bream boy, Brian was at Lydney Grammar School before working at the Pine End works stripping veneer from oak, walnut and foreign timber. Moving to the Princess Royal colliery he was employed as a linesman, an assistant to

Brian Johns holding his dowsing rods.

the pit surveyor and later as an underground haulage driver. When the Forest's pits faced closure he became a policeman with Birmingham City Police but on every possible occasion during his twenty-eight years' service he returned each weekend to the Forest and his wife Saxon's Blakeney cottage birthplace. On retirement there ten years ago he discovered an interest in Forest history. 'We hadn't been taught it at school and it was the old story of familiarity breeds contempt. Looking around when I had the liberty to do so literally opened my eyes. History and the Forest go hand in hand, it's all around you.' He is now vice-chairman of the Awre Parish Council which includes Blakeney, and a trustee of the Dean Heritage Centre

When taking up dowsing he tested the accuracy of the rods' reactions over well surveyed sites. 'I made many mistakes, but eventually I mastered the art,' he says, adding that a practice scan at Littledean Hall located a previously unknown track and adjacent building. After a survey of the route of the ancient lane alongside the Bideford brook, a dig uncovered Roman pottery and a rare black glass bead now on display in the Heritage Centre. When he undertook a survey of Blakeney Hill he and colleagues identified hundreds of medieval charcoal hearths. 'In 238 acres I discovered 233 hearth sites. This suggests that each acre of woodland, coppiced on a twenty-year rotation, produced enough wood for charcoaling to smelt one load of iron ore.'

In his *New History* of the Forest, Cyril Hart reproduces Brian's dowsing survey of Cannop House. He is currently surveying the line of the Dean Road from Lydney northwards through the Forest towards Weston-under-Penyard and the Roman iron-smelting centre at Ariconium (present-day Bromsash). The date of the exposed cobble track at Blackpool Brook bridge is disputed but the existence of a Roman route is virtually beyond doubt, so many Roman artefacts having been found nearby. He is also engaged in work at Rodmore, a Roman site currently being excavated by members of the Dean Archaeological Group, of which he is chairman. You want to invite yourself along to observe a dowsing session but Brian forestalls the idea. 'I concentrate better on my own, because the results are better without distractions.' As for the Dean Road he comments, 'I have some possible indications of a dating. Whether that upsets some people we will have to wait and see.'

Making life easier for everyone interested in Forest history was the publication in 1996 of the definitive *Victoria County History* volume covering the Forest of Dean. It was primarily the seven years' achievement of Dr Nicholas Herbert (fifty-six), historian at Gloucestershire County Council's Records Office in Gloucester. After school in Cheltenham, Nicholas read history at Reading University and for the last thirty-two years has been preparing new titles for the epic project which began, as its name suggests, as long ago as 1899. Of an eventual twenty planned Gloucestershire volumes, eight have so far been published. If this seems slow progress, it is far more advanced than many other English counties, Gloucestershire being fortunate that the county council continued to support it in conjunction with the Cheltenham and Gloucester College of Higher Education. The Forest is doubly fortunate in being an area

Gloucestershire Records Office historian Dr Nicholas Herbert, editor and co-author of the Victoria County History *volume on the Forest of Dean, with an old Forest map from the Dean Heritage Centre's Gage Library treasure trove.*

chosen for treatment, given precedence even over the completion of the Cotswolds, which Nicholas is now working on.

The earlier Volume X covering the Westbury and Whitstone Hundreds, published in 1972, was edited and co-written by his then boss Dr C.R. Elrington – Nicholas contributing the chapters on Westbury and Tidenham. For the latest volume, Nicholas as editor was assisted by co-author Dr John Jurica. Together they survey, in 440 large double-column pages, the Bledisloe and St Briavels Hundreds and the formerly extra-parochial Forest. For a scholarly work it is lightly written. Their descriptions of the area's settlement, industry, administration, social and church life and education bring alive the places and their people. For their research has not been solely a desk job among the archives. 'There is no substitute for fieldwork, matching evidence from documents to what you can see on the ground,' Nicholas points out. 'At the same time all the church records are here and landowners and solicitors have deposited their old files.' He is particularly pleased that nowadays his efforts are read by a wider audience than adults interested in local history. 'Local studies are now an important part of the school curriculum, so the county history is the schoolchildren's natural starting point as well.' The next volume due after the Cotswolds will be on the Newent area.

CHAPTER 11

Mansions and Dynasties

'Four years ago I couldn't spell the word "archaeology",' confesses John Cotterill, bluff Brummie manager of the St Briavels Castle youth hostel. 'Then, on a freezing January morning, with snowflakes falling around, you are standing in the mud looking at a stretch of old wall uncovered by the archaeologists and feel very excited. I am very aware we are custodians of a very important historical building. At the same time it's good it isn't just an ancient monument and is serving a useful present-day purpose.'

A former telephone engineer, John and wife Eileen took up hiking when they had children and wanted to get away from Birmingham for weekends and holidays. 'Then twenty years ago I saw this advertisement for a job as warden of the English Bicknor youth hostel, applied and was accepted. It was a lovely place but there were three separate buildings and road access was very difficult.' After several years there and then postings elsewhere around Britain he and Eileen were appointed to St Briavels five years ago. Since then he has become an expert on every nook and cranny of the castle and a guide to the groups visiting each week.

The original castle was probably built in the early 1100s by the Forest's bailiff, appointed by Henry I (1100–1135) to warden the woodlands. Like the other small castles of this vintage around the Dean plateau's edge, it was most likely a wooden hall on a mound with this and a courtyard surrounded by a timber palisade and ditch. By 1130, Miles of Gloucester was warden of the Forest with the castle as its administrative centre. The title of Constable of the castle was co-joined to that of Warden but although it was strongly fortified in these and later years it saw little serious military action.

It was on the other hand an important munitions-making centre, the Crown being as much interested in the Forest's iron-making capacity as in its hunting facilities. Successive monarchs ordered a range of metal objects – horseshoes, nails, shovels and later crossbow bolts – for campaigns in the Borders, France, the Holy Land and Ireland. In order to protect the woodlands which provided charcoal for smelting and forging (and the revenue therefrom), the Crown applied severe restrictions on the cutting of timber and iron-making activities. The clash between industrialists, large and small, became the recurrent theme of Forest history, the timber later becoming as valued for shipbuilding purposes as for fuel.

Henry II (1154–89) and King John (1199–1216) are recorded as being frequent visitors to the Forest, a stone keep probably being erected on the castle's south side during the former's reign. Financial records from the latter's time show building works which would have included the hall block and the stone curtain wall. During Henry III's years (1216–72) the weapon-making business expanded. 'In [1228] John Malemort and his brother William the Smith, and William the Fletcher were sent to the castle to produce quarrels [crossbow bolts] there [and] by 1233 were producing 12,000 quarrels in a 120-day period,' records Mike Salter in his booklet guide to St Briavels castle. It continues with hair-raising details of the even greater quantities required by Edward I (1272–1307), who also ordered the construction of the great twin-towered gatehouse on the castle's north side.

Edward II (1307–27) continued the rebuilding and for the siege of Berwick in 1310 ordered up archers and miners – one of the possible origins of the Forest miners' privileges later described as stretching back 'time out of mind'. The castle continued to be active under Edward III (1327–77) but the grant of the Forest and castle to Thomas Duke of Gloucester by his uncle Richard II (1377–99) suggests it

Present-day custodians of St Briavels Castle, youth hostel manager John Cotterill and wife Eileen with assistant Chris Bloor in the courtyard between gatehouse (right) and chapel (left).

was of less strategic importance than formerly, though still a venue for various local courts and a prison.

John Cotterill shows off the cell in the west gatehouse tower, its walls scratched with prisoners' laments, and the grim dungeon reached by a trapdoor in the floor of the east tower. By Elizabethan times the place was described as being half demolished, only the upper storey solar and chapel being usable. These survive in more or less their original form, having been used as the parish school in the later nineteenth century. Rebuilding and modernization created a private residence in the early twentieth century, after which it was taken on by the predecessor of English Heritage and leased to the Youth Hostels Association in 1947. The courtyard is open to visitors between Easter and the end of autumn – 'except I don't close the gates, so in reality they can come in almost any time within reason,' says John.

Although an ecclesiastical building, the early history of Flaxley Abbey was as closely associated with the first Plantagenets as St Briavels itself. During the civil war between Henry I's daughter Matilda and her cousin Stephen (1135–54), Miles of Gloucester supported the former – together with her half-brother Earl Robert. During a lull in the twelve-year-long hostilities in 1143 Miles, by now Earl of Hereford, was out hunting in the Flaxley valley. In a re-enactment of

Flaxley Abbey, home of Catharina Boevey (1670–1726) and of her Crawley-Boevey successors until the 1960s.

William II's assassination in the New Forest, he was killed by an arrow fired by an unknown assailant.

Matilda, having married Geoffrey Plantagenet, Count of Anjou, had retired abroad, leaving her young son Henry in the care of Earl Robert. The latter undertook to provide a memorial to Miles in the then popular form of a new monastery. Already in residence at Tintern since 1131, the Cistercians were invited to consider taking on the proposed new foundation. An inspection party arrived from the mother house at Cîteaux in Burgundy and approved the site, but demanded a guarantee of the deed of land and an adequate endowment. Travelling to Cîteaux, Earl Robert was able to provide this and gained acceptance of the plans which included a royal hall seating two hundred. Work went ahead, Henry laying the foundation stone at a lavish ceremony in 1148. Robert having died in the meantime, the abbey's grandiose opening in 1151 was arranged by Thomas Becket, later Henry's Chancellor and Archbishop of Canterbury, and Earl Roger.

The star of the event was the eighteen-year-old Henry, who in the three days of ensuing festivities joined a party invited by Walter de Clifford across river from his manor at Frampton. Here Henry met Walter's fifteen-year-old daughter Rosamund. The pair were mutually attracted and marriage would have followed, except that a greater dynastic alliance presented itself. The king of France divorced Eleanor of Aquitaine, not at all to her displeasure, and eligible suitors galloped to her court from all over Europe – Henry among them. Despite the ten years or so age gap, she chose the inheritor of the Anjou lands adjoining her own, who was also the likely future king of England.

They married in 1152. Henry was accepted as heir to the throne in the following year and he was crowned as Henry II on Stephen's death in the year after. Eleanor bore him four sons but at the same time Henry had embarked on an affair with 'the fair Rosamund' which produced two further sons – William 'Longsword', later Earl of Salisbury, and Geoffrey, later Archbishop of Canterbury. Astonishingly, since his legitimate children were a quarrelsome brood, the half-brothers got on well with them.

Their father was a frequent visitor to Flaxley for business and pleasure. The nearby Newnham, with its port providing convenient passage to Bristol, France and Ireland as well as the ferry across the Severn, was the centre of many of

Henry's activities. Henry launched his 1171 invasion of Ireland from here, well supplied with Forest-made armaments. Encouraged by his mother, eldest son Henry took the opportunity – fuelled by widespread dismay at the murder of Thomas Becket in 1170 – to revolt. The Scots invaded England and the Welsh joined in. Henry, having re-established control and a reconciliation with his son (but not his wife), organized a grand ceremony of loyalty pledges at Gloucester in 1175.

Its aftermath was less successful. On the death of her mother shortly afterwards, Rosamund became a nun; Henry junior died; Henry's sons Richard and John continued to foment rebellion in England and the former's designated French territory; and Eleanor was locked up at Banbury. Henry somehow coped with all this fairly equably. Various episodes relating to the Forest are recounted by his friend and the most appealing of eye-witness historians, the monk Gerald of Wales. He includes in his travelogues (available in Penguin Books) a hilarious account of the dispute between Flaxley's abbot and Newnham's vicar. The more modern version of Flaxley's history is provided by Baden Watkins in his endlessly fascinating *The Story of Flaxley Abbey* (1985); he bought the abbey in 1960 and masterminded its subsequent restoration.

On Henry's death and burial at the great Fontevraud Abbey in Anjou his son Richard 'Lionheart' (1189–99) succeeded to the throne. He visited Flaxley Abbey to enjoy the hunting and check out revenues from its already established iron-making furnaces and forges before departing on the Third Crusade which his father had wished to join. His brother King John was a more assiduous visitor to the Forest and Flaxley, as was John's son Henry III (1216–77), who became the abbey's most generous of benefactors since its foundation. It was thus ironic that the abbey was a temporary redoubt for the dissident Earl of Pembroke who, having failed to regain his Chepstow castle, sought refuge here in 1234.

Henry's troops laid siege to the abbey but for two months refrained from attacking such a sanctified place. The Earl was eventually allowed to flee to Ireland where he was later killed by the king's allies. The abbey was awarded almost a thousand acres of the Forest's woodland, still known as Abbot's Wood. Despite this, in the century ruled by the three King Edwards (1277–1377), the abbey provoked frequent protests from the Constable and Warden of the Forest for its excessive felling of timber. Edward III nevertheless retained sufficient affection for the place inaugurated by the first of his line to fund the 1353 rebuilding of the Abbot's Room in the form which can be seen today.

The abbey declined in importance in the years leading up to Henry VIII's dissolution of this and other monasteries in 1536. Already Constable of St Briavels Castle as well as Constable of the Tower of London, Sir William Kingston was awarded the deconsecrated premises as reward for his efficient handling of the beheading of Henry's wife Anne Boleyn. His son Sir Anthony Kingston, 'the Terrible Marshall', was knighted by Edward IV, organized the burning at the stake of Bishop Hooper of Gloucester under the Catholic Queen Mary, and then switched allegiance by plotting to replace her by her sister Elizabeth. Arrested at Flaxley, he was escorted towards the Tower of London and certain execution but jumped his horse over Staines bridge into the Thames and drowned.

His descendants led a more peaceful existence until their sale of the property to the Dutch-born Boevey family of businessmen in 1647. William Boevey brought his fifteen-year-old bride Catharina here in 1687. When he died seven years later she became known as 'the perverse widow', her literary friends Addison and Steele describing her thus – thinly disguised – in their accounts of her refusal of suitors in their *Tatler* journal. Bluestocking, philanthropist and evangelical, she supported the growth of the Sunday school movement and Society for the Promotion of Christian Knowledge, while in Flaxley she was a benefactor of the local people and in particular their children. On her death in 1726 she was commemorated by an elaborate monument in Westminster Abbey and an effusive plaque in Flaxley church installed by her lifelong friend Mary Pope (who gave her name to Pope's Hill).

After the death of her husband Catharina completed the laying out of an elaborate formal garden around the house, similar to the Dutch-style water garden preserved at Westbury-on-Severn. She also supervised the ironworks operating on the Flaxley stream in the tradition of the Forest gentry's role as active industrialists. The estate passed to her husband's relative, Thomas Crawley, who added the Boevey suffix to his surname. For two centuries and more the Crawley-Boeveys were local dignitaries, active in civic and political life, and energetic 'improvers'. Sir Thomas Crawley-Boevey (d. 1818), High Sheriff of Gloucestershire, rebuilt the house in handsome Georgian style after a fire in 1777. His son, also Sir Thomas (d. 1847), built the village school. In the time of Sir Martin Crawley-Boevey (d. 1862) the new St Mary's church rose on a new site to the designs of the leading architect Sir George Gilbert Scott.

Plaques adorning the church walls follow the family's later military tradition. Martin Crawley-Boevey (d. 1883) is noted as having won the DSO and MC. Thomas, a Royal Navy sub-lieutenant, went down with the submarine *Tigris* in the Mediterranean in 1943. After the war the family sold off 500 acres of woodland to the Forestry Commission and in 1960 the house and 200 acres of land was acquired by industrialist Baden Watkins. His wife Phyllis brought in notable theatre artist Oliver Messel for extensive restoration and redecoration. The refectory and Abbot's Room of the west wing survive essentially in their original form. While the house is not open to the public, the church can be visited by obtaining a key from the blacksmith's almost opposite.

Although the present Lydney Park house is of Victorian vintage, the estate represents the continuity of two dynasties covering over four centuries. Bristol merchant John Winter (d. 1546), with a fleet of armed merchantmen trading with the Levant, advised Henry VIII on the forming of a permanent navy and, as Ralph Anstis recounts in *Four Personalities from the Forest of Dean*, was appointed 'first paymaster of his new Navy and captain of one of its finest warships'. As with many Bristolians before and after, he sought a home across the water and settled in Lydney. Also joining the navy, his son John was sufficiently successful to buy the Lydney manor in about 1560, gain a knighthood in 1573, become one of Gloucestershire's two MPs, and be appointed admiral – in which capacity he fought against the Armada, dying in the following year.

During the encounter his son Edward, a godson of Queen Elizabeth, was captured. Having been ransomed, Edward – now a substantial landowner – became a courtier. Elizabeth made him Master of the Horse, high sheriff of Gloucestershire, and Constable of St Briavels castle. Having been knighted in 1595 he also twice served as MP. In the new reign of James I the Winter family, as strong Catholics, were implicated in the Gunpowder Plot, after which three of his cousins were executed. Edward concentrated on his estate, which by now included not only the manors around Lydney but also that of Purton. He built one of the Forest's first blast furnaces using water power and a forge alongside, thus launching Lydney's industrial future.

Inheriting on his father's death in 1619, John Winter (1602–c. 1685) built or acquired further ironworks (including Gunn's Mill), married into the aristocracy, and became private secretary to Charles I's French-born queen, Henrietta Maria. In the Forest he supported Charles's attempts to enclose the woodlands to protect their timber. After suppressing riots led by John Williams (alias Skeffington), which lasted intermittently from 1628 to 1632, he was appointed one of Gloucestershire's deputy lieutenants. In 1639, having effectively bought the Forest from the king, he continued with the enclosures while felling even those trees intended for naval use. 'He was now the second greatest ironmaster in England,' writes Ralph Anstis in *Four Personalities*. 'He had six furnaces and eight forges in the Forest himself, and he and Benedict Hall, a rival ironmaster who operated on the other side of the Forest, between them now controlled almost three quarters of the woods in the area, nine of the fifteen furnaces and fifteen of the twenty forges.'

When Parliament defied the king, Winter was forced to give up the woods. When civil war broke out he attempted to defend the Forest against Colonel Edward Massey, governor of Gloucester. During the next three years he fought bitter skirmishes at Newnham, Huntley, Beachley, Lancaut and his own White Cross House, which he burnt down rather than leave to the enemy. Forced to flee across the Wye on several occasions, he was appointed governor of Chepstow Castle but the Royalist cause was wavering. Having already accompanied Queen Henrietta on a hazardous escape across the Channel to France, he sought refuge there until after the king's execution.

His estate was confiscated and when he returned he was imprisoned in the Tower of London for four years. He bought back his own land but at the Restoration had to negotiate for the renewal of his lease of woodland and the king's furnaces, such as those at Lydbrook and Parkend. This achieved he set about felling the woodland to the extent that it was alleged that only 200 trees remained of the 30,000 he had pledged to preserve. His activities were halted by a 1668 Act of Parliament which decreed that half of the formal Forest – or some 11,000 acres of woodland – should be protected by enclosure.

The rest of his life is obscure, his date of death and grave being unknown. He had already handed over the Lydney estate to his son William, who passed it on to his brother Charles, who built a new Lydney Park mansion near Aylburton in about 1692. On the latter's death in 1698 it went to his widow Frances. When she died in 1720 it was sold to Benjamin Bathurst MP. As well as representing in turn

MP for Monmouth (1790–96) and for other constituencies till 1822, Charles Bragge assumed the Bathurst name on inheriting the Lydney Park estate from his uncle in 1804, and was Chancellor of the Duchy of Lancaster, 1812–23.

the constituencies of Cirencester, Colchester and Monmouth, he was father of thirty-six children – his first wife dying after giving birth to her twenty-second. None of the sons produced surviving male heirs so the estate was inherited – after his wife's death – by the nephew of Poole Bathurst (d. 1792), Charles Bragge.

Bragge, who later took the Bathurst name, was MP for Monmouth from 1790 to 1796. In an extraordinary 32-year-long parliamentary career he sat throughout the French Revolution and Napoleonic wars and their fraught aftermath. As MP for Bristol (1796–1812) he was appointed to the government as Secretary for War in 1803/4, inheriting Lydney Park in the same year. While MP for Bodmin (1812–18) he became Chancellor of the Duchy of Lancaster (1812–23), a post he continued to hold as MP for Harwich (1818–22). A small oval portrait hanging over the dining room fireplace of the present Lydney Park is his modest memorial – though he enjoyed a decade of retirement until his death in 1831.

His son Charles concentrated on more local affairs. He became a Verderer, is praised by Nicholls for his philanthropy, and dying childless in 1863 was succeeded by his brother the Revd William Hiley Bathurst (d. 1877). He initiated the building of the present mansion further up the hill, amid its deer park and below the knoll occupied by the Roman Temple

The first Viscount Bledisloe, Charles Bathurst (1867–1958).

of Nodens, which was inherited by his son Charles (d. 1907). Owner of almost all Lydney's land and much of its industries, Charles was the epitome of a late Victorian landowner – commercial but benevolent. He and other local industrialists and benefactors laid the basis of Lydney's present-day civic infrastructure, and he encouraged his son Charles to follow the same path.

Charles (1867–1958), later the 1st Viscount Bledisloe, has previously been mentioned by Professor Emery as turning up to discuss with the latter's local schoolteacher father the affairs of Aylburton Parish Council. A full account of his life as one of the Forest's most influential people would occupy a whole book. Dr Cyril Hart, fortunately, provided a swift but meticulous blueprint in his celebration of Lord Bledisloe's ninetieth birthday, when the Queen and the Duke of Edinburgh planted an oak outside the Speech House to mark the occasion. Son Benjamin was succeeded by the present 3rd Lord Bledisloe, Christopher Bathurst. Claiming to be 'England's oldest house', Littledean Hall has a Roman temple in its grounds overlooking the River Severn, a basement of Saxon origin and a medieval kitchen area where new owners John and Sheila Christopher talked of their restoration plans for the mostly seventeenth-century structure. It is the only historic house in the Forest open to visitors, and the Christophers are hoping to increase its attractions. 'We aren't aiming to recreate it totally in the seventeenth-century period,' John explains. 'The idea is more to show it as it would have been lived in as a small country house at the turn of the century, with an accumulation of furniture from different periods.'

Having been with the Brayne family for three centuries, it was acquired in 1612 by Charles Bridgeman of Poulton Court, Awre, who built the grandiose northern wing with splendidly wood-panelled walls. It was the scene of a vicious skirmish during the Civil War when two Royalist officers were slain in the dining room, contributing to the tales of various ghosts haunting the place. It is atmospheric enough without such yarns, a priest hole at ceiling level and a camouflaged chapel attesting to the Catholic sympathies of its occupants.

These were, after the Restoration, the Pyrkes of Abenhall. H.G. Nicholls describes how Thomas Pyrke was appointed a Regarder at the time of Charles II's attempts to regulate Forest affirs. Son Nathaniel, who

With Roman temple in the grounds, Saxon undercroft and a Jacobean interior, Littledean Hall is now owned by balloonists John and Sheila Christopher – and their quartet of cats.

married a daughter of Duncombe Colchester of Westbury and The Wilderness, and was a Verderer, as was his son Thomas. Later Pyrkes were JPs as well as Verderers, Joseph Pyrke being attacked during the 1795 corn riots.

Duncombe Pyrke added the seventeenth-century style northern façade and entrance in 1852, diverting the road outside the grounds. The property passed out of the family in 1896 but the grounds as well as the house itself retain their estately appearance, with a row of ancient chestnut trees lining the drive and a Victorian garden dropping down towards the village. The Christophers were planning to pursue their balloon business from here, with the prevailing south-west wind carrying craft over the Vale of Leadon. (A year later the winds had proved so contrary that only one flight had been possible.)

Standing in front of Clearwell Castle, new owner Harry Bramer explained that the building – sadly run down in recent years – had attracted him. Having previously restored a Tudor manor house in Essex as a venue for weddings, he was now booked at weekends for years ahead and was looking for another location. 'As soon as I saw it I knew it was ideal. It's a house full of character, and with wonderful grounds. It needed a lot of work doing to it but it's all more or less finished now.'

Previously called Clearwell Court, its predecessor was the village manor house occupied in the early fifteenth century by the Greyndours. The Greyndour daughter

Its great estate was broken up in 1907 but Clearwell Castle has recently been restored to its eighteenth-century grandeur by new owner Harry Bramer.

married Thomas Baynham, and the daughter of a later Thomas married Sir William Throckmorton (d. 1628) to whom the estate was passed. His son Sir Baynham Throckmorton was Sir John Winter's great rival in Forest affairs but his estate was also confiscated during the Civil War. Re-purchased, it was sold by his son's daughter to Francis Wyndham in 1698.

Thomas Wyndham built the Court as one of the earliest mansions in the neo-Gothic fashion in about 1728. An early nineteenth-century Wyndham daughter married Windham Henry Quin who took the name of Wyndham and later inherited the Irish earldom of Dunraven. His widow, the Countess of Dunraven, undertook lavish building work in the house and village, including St Peter's parish church. When the house passed out of the Wyndham family the Court and estate were sold off at a spectacular auction in 1907.

The mansion went to Colonel Charles Vereker, was largely destroyed by fire in 1939, partially restored by the Colonel, but left derelict after his death in 1947. The son of a former gardener, Frank Yeates, took it on and refurbished it gradually until selling it as a hotel in the early 1980s. The venue is now booked well ahead, the old library being a resplendent marriage room and evening receptions being held in the vaulted basement.

At Blaisdon Hall it was moving out day for the monks who had occupied it for the past sixty years. By 1933 the mansion had severely deteriorated and was sold off at auction to the Salesian Order, which runs schools for underprivileged children. They are taught practical trades such as carpentry, tailoring, engineering and farming. It was also a seminary for thirty trainee priests but these departed when the Hall became a special school for boys with educational and behavioural difficulties in 1950.

By 1993 the complement of pupils was down to nineteen and the school closed at the end of the 1994 summer term. 'The Government obviously prefers to spend money on keeping them in prison later in their lives,' said the rector, Father Sean Murray, sadly. He was clearing his desk and handed me *A Short History of Blaisdon* by former headmaster Father Pat Kenna. It described how the house was built in the 1870s by William Crawshay, 'the Iron King of the Forest', who had rebuilt his own mansion at Oaklands Park in 1850.

Having largely contributed to the restoration of Blaisdon's St Michael and All Angels parish church in 1867, Crawshay noticed that the land alongside was possibly an excellent location for a house for his son Edwin, who was running the family's Lightmoor mine. Though the house was completed, in Elizabethan Renaissance style, in 1876, Edwin seemed unenthusiastic. He let it to a tenant and then defaulted on the mortgage payments. The property was repossessed by the banks and sold to Peter Stubbs, a file manufacturer from Warrington.

The estate included the whole of the village apart from the Red Hart public house, amounting to 1,278 acres. Stubbs established a nationally famous stud of fifty horses at Stud Farm. Known as 'the Squire', he built a new village school, now the village hall. His daughter married Colin McIver from Warrington and on her father's death in 1905 the couple inherited. They continued the work of creating the model village, replacing tumbledown labourers' cottages with new semi-detached houses.

Built for iron master Edwin Crawshay, Blaisdon Hall was occupied until recently by the youth training centre run by Salesian brothers such as Fathers Pat Kenna and Aidan Murray.

With a lordly attitude towards their tenants, Mrs McIver objected to being stared at by the village children as she drove by in her pioneering motor car, so all the windows in the houses are high off the ground. When her husband died in 1927, having been High Sheriff of Gloucester, she departed. One of the Salesians arriving here after its purchase was Brother Alan Garman, who stayed on when he retired to help the pupils in their leisure activities. Aged seventy-seven, he had just that morning cycled off to catch a train to his native Ireland to continue his retirement. Father Murray had himself been there thirty years – 'almost half my life,' he mused – and was unsure what his future would be. The Hall was acquired as an annex for the Hartpury College and its grounds welcome the public on special occasions.

CHAPTER 12

Hotels, Public Houses and Affrays

Harry Kear stands in front of the Speech House, proud new lessee of a building that was once centre of Forest affairs. Built in the 1670s to replace Kensley Lodge where the Attachment Court, later known as the Verderers' Court, was held from at least 1338, the King's Lodge (as it was originally called) was one of half a dozen constructed during the post–Civil War reorganization of the Forest into six 'walks'. It also became the venue for the previously peripatetic mine law court regulating mining practice within the Forest, thus gaining the name of Speech House. The court more or less ended in the eighteenth century when a corrupt official broke into its muniments chest and stole its records, but the Verderers' Court still meets here, as does the Forest of Dean Rotary Club. It was thus a natural target for rioters demonstrating against the enclosures erected to protect new growing plantations from being severely damaged by cottagers' free-ranging animals in 1688.

The Foresters have a long history of insubordination. In 1356 the Gainer family of St Briavels and Aylburton operated as an armed gang within the Forest, having refused service as archers in the king's army in the north. In 1429 there were complaints of Foresters attacking and robbing ships passing by Newnham, repeated in Henry VIII's reign when 'there came out multitudes of people from Bledisloe and Westbury with great riot and strength in manner of warre as enemys of a strange land'. When Sir John Winter erected enclosures around the woodlands serving his furnaces, the latter were destroyed in 1631. The same year saw an attack in the north of the Forest by a five hundred-strong mob on enclosures around Mailscot wood. Similar incidents occurred while the Forest was being administered by the Parliamentarian Colonel Wade during the Protectorate.

'The injuries done by the mob to the Speech House and two of the other lodges in 1688 . . . seem to account for the contemporary remark of Dr Parsons that "the inhabitants are, some of them, a sort of robustic, wild people that must be civilised by good discipline and government,"' Nicholls notes. There were serious outbreaks of violence during the French Revolution and Napoleonic wars when in 1795 Mitcheldean's corn market was attacked in bread riots. Ships at Awre were boarded and ransacked. The squire of Littledean Hall, magistrate Richard Pyrke, led a troop of cavalry which captured five of the pillagers, two of whom were later hanged. There were further disturbances in 1801, before the even more widespread outbreaks of 1831.

The Speech House, seat of the Verderers Court, has recently been acquired by Harry Kear, fourth generation master-baker.

By 1841 the Speech House was redundant and was handed over to its watchman to run as an inn. Enlarged into a hotel in 1882, it was lodging place for Sir Charles Dilke and his large party when he came to the Forest in 1889 to prepare for his election to Parliament. The adjacent field was used for the Miners' Demonstration each July when as many as ten thousand people led by brass bands paraded here. While families enjoyed picnics and games, the men spent the afternoon listening to lengthy speeches by miners' leaders, such as Timothy Mountjoy, and those such as Dilke, the Forest's MP from 1892 until his death in 1911.

Elections in the earlier period were often boisterous. On the 1874 election day Liberal supporters gathered outside Cinderford's Fleece Inn where the Tories had established their headquarters and threatened to burn it down. When the landlord appeared waving a pistol they set off down the street smashing the windows of shops and inns whose owners were suspected of being Tory voters. The police, several of whom were injured, sought Timothy Mountjoy's assistance in dispersing the rioters, numbering between two and three hundred. Pulling an old bill out of his pocket he read a pretended telegram saying that troops were arriving within the hour.

Harry Kear acquired the hotel from Trust House Forte in 1998, he and his family having disposed of their bakery business, which began at the Yorkley

Royal Forest of Dean Rotary Club members at their monthly Speech House gathering. From left, front: the late Harold Bright (journalist), Tim Mason (President 1994), Basil Marfell (founder member and secretary); back: Douglas Marfell (founder member), John Ball (treasurer for eighteen years), Dave Phillips (Speech House development manager), David Bennett and Derrick Langford (founder member).

cottage of his great grandmother. 'She used to bake the family's bread, putting cabbage leaves underneath to keep the loaves clean and get a bit of steam in the oven,' Harry recounts. 'It was so popular that neighbours came round to buy it, so she developed what became a cottage industry.' It expanded under his father and grandfather, a bakery being built on the site which still survives as premises of a food firm in which Harry also has an interest.

'I used to leave Lydney Grammar School and look across at the district council offices and think to myself, "I'd like to have that one day,"' he says over coffee in the hotel foyer. He started work in the family firm doing anything from driving bread delivery vans to serving in the Bream breadshop, until concentrating on sales. 'We bought the first Starbake Ltd premises at Newport, making sliced bread, in 1983,' he says in charting the firm's swift expansion. Other Starbakes followed in Yorkshire, Cumbria, Lancashire and Buckinghamshire, with their headquarters in the old council offices. His brother Ronald meanwhile built up his Featherstone's Hot Bread Shops from his Bream bakery base, while sister Brenda has her Mrs Pastries shop in Monmouth's Monnow Street.

When the family sold the company, Harry, an active Rotarian, bought the Speech House not just for sentimental reasons but as a flagship for a mini-chain of hotel-restaurants he planned to open. Leading off on a tour, he showed the Verderers' Court room occupied by the à la carte restaurant, the cheaper brasserie rooms installed within a month of his taking over, the two grandest bedrooms with their four-poster beds from Flaxley Abbey, and in the garden outside, the lawn where he plans to erect a summertime marquee catering for casual customers, especially families. It seemed somehow appropriate that the Forest's most symbolic building was once again under local management, the ground landlord being still the Forestry Commission.

Coleford's Angel Hotel was centre of town life for three centuries from Elizabethan times and possibly earlier. An inn is shown on the site in a 1608 map and a 1653 document refers to 'the Inn at Coleford'. This could mean the town's other inn, the Fleur de Lys, later the Plume of Feathers and today the Feathers Hotel, but is more likely to denote the Angel – also known as the Great Inn. It

Coleford's Angel Hotel, location of a Civil War battle and the commital of Warren James by local magistrates.

was around this redoubt that the Battle of Coleford was fought in 1643, when Royalist forces from their Raglan base marched against the town held by the Parliamentarians' Colonel Sir John Berrow. After house-to-house fighting they won the day but at the considerable loss of senior officers. Among those shot dead was their general Sir Richard Lawley (supposedly by a sniper from the King's Head), a captain of dragoons, a lieutenant of horse and a major who died of his wounds in Highmeadow House after the battle. The Parliamentary dead included Sir John Winter's brother, buried at Lydney's St Mary's.

The Forest's prevailing neutrality during hostilities paid off at the Restoration. Coleford gained the rights to a weekly market in 1661 and it gradually became the Forest's *de facto* capital. Two other inns, the Old White Hart and King's Head, served an increasing local and visiting clientele. But it was at the Angel that the Excise installed their local office, with the job of supervising local brewing and collecting beer duty. This might have something to do with the fact that it was owned by the Halls of Highmeadow, whose influence in government was considerable. But sometimes not influential enough, for as Cyril Hart records in his Coleford history, the Excise officers were moved elsewhere, although they returned by 1792 when the inn also housed the Post Office.

The hotel was rebuilt in the early years of the new century, incorporating the magnificent bow windows from the recently demolished Highmeadow House. The magistrates relocated here from St Briavels, alternating their sessions between the Angel and Lydney's Feathers Hotel. Meetings of local and outside entrepreneurs were held here to promote new enterprises such as tramways. But resentment grew among the commoners against Edward Machen's forest ordinances and the incursions of 'foreigners' into local iron and coal mining industries. In 1831 the unassuming but doughty Warren James found himself leading two thousand fellow cottagers in night-time attacks on the walls and fences of the enclosures. On the other side of the Forest, rioters were at the same time attacking Bilson House, the home of Aaron Goold, Edward Protheroe's agent and manager of his Cinderford coal mines.

Troops were summoned to Coleford from Monmouth but these turned out to be a motley bunch, derided by onlookers as 'the ragged regiment'. They were followed by more serious cavalry, the authorities' panic being demonstrated by the assembly of local notables including the Duke of Beaufort, his son the Marquis of Worcester, the High Sheriff of Gloucestershire and local magistrates from the Forest's great families. Warren James was found hiding in a mine shaft, captured and brought to the Angel where the magistrates committed him to Gloucester jail. At the Assizes he was found guilty of riot and condemned to death. Reprieved after the intercession of local worthies he was instead transported to the convict colony of Tasmania. Though granted a pardon in 1836, he lacked the money to pay for his return voyage and died in Hobart five years later.

The Angel hosted many civic, political and business gatherings in Victorian times. A committee was established here in 1840 to launch the company which built the gasworks and lit the town's streets, the hotel's then landlord being of sufficient consequence to subscribe for shares and be appointed company treasurer. Queen Victoria's diamond jubilee was feted with a dinner in the Old

Today's civic worthies in the Angel's old bar. From left: Bart Venner, Forest district council leader, Bill Hobman, council chairman and wife Valerie, also a councillor, and outgoing leader Bruce Hogan.

White Hart and an evening dance at the Angel. The militia drilled here, presumably in the stable block, until the drill hall was built which later became The Studio cinema. A present-day cameo of its past civic role was provided in 1996 following that year's local elections. At the end of the new council's inaugural evening meeting, its leading figures sat around a table in the Angel's street-front bar (rescued from temporary ignominy as a pizza restaurant). They consisted of veteran council chairman Bill Hobman and his wife, herself a councillor, outgoing leader Bruce Hogan and newly elected leader Bart Venner.

❖ ❖ ❖

The history of this and some four hundred other past and present Forest pubs has been compiled but not yet published by Cinderford's Ray Allen, retired history teacher of the one-time Double View school. Born in Hastings, a good birthplace for any historian, Ray was reluctant to follow in the family's teaching footsteps and after school worked for three years for a small airline company. Having belatedly done a teacher training course, he saw a job vacancy advertised in Cinderford. 'I thought it would be nice to live in the Cotswolds,' he chuckles, as we go through his files on a summer evening outside Littledean's Belfry inn, formerly the George. 'Geography was never my strong point.' He met his future wife Pat when they were both working on building the Biblins log cabin. She is nowadays diocesan officer for readers at Gloucester cathedral. From the 1960s, he was an enthusiastic supporter of the town's rugby club and its chairman for five years into the early 1990s.

'The problem in finding out about Forest pubs is that systematic records only began with the great licensing act of 1869, and that police records for the Lydney district have somehow disappeared,' he explains. 'Records are also subject to a fifty-year confidentiality ban on publication, although that is becoming less important as the years go by.' To illustrate what has become almost a hidden history of the Forest's fabric, he describes the dozen or so pubs which once existed in Littledean, where only the Belfry, the King's Head and the Littledean House Hotel now survive. The disconcerting fact about Littledean is that the old

Historian Ray Allen at Littledean's Belfry, formerly the George.

thoroughfare went in a completely different direction from today's main road. For centuries the busiest route was the one climbing up past Littledean Hall from Newnham and turning right at the present junction with Broad Street rather than left towards Cinderford. Travellers went downhill past the parish church to the corner where the road continued below Chestnut Wood to the Flaxley valley at Green Bottom and then to Mitcheldean, onward destinations being Ross and Hereford.

Thus Littledean's numerous pubs clustered on the old Gloucester Road, now Church Street. Opposite the recently resurrected King's Head a house bears a panel announcing that it was 'The Victoria', demonstrating the complexity of Ray's task. 'I can't find any record of it,' he shakes his head. But he has lots of information on the King's Head, the Cross Keys opposite, the Swan, the Greyhound down the Gloucester Road and the Belfry itself, punningly renamed after its rebuilding by the Bell family – fellow rugby enthusiasts – and happily retaining the George's public bar where old locals congregate. Towards midnight (I was a resident for the night) Ray admitted he was 'not really a pub person – pubs were just a sideline that happened to crop up'. I bemoaned the fact that there seemed to be no comprehensive record of Forest collieries. 'Oh, I've done those as well,' he responds, 'and their file is twice as thick.'

Once Dean Parva to Mitcheldean's Dean Magna, Littledean was the obvious location for the astonishing gaol, a police station until 1972 and magistrates' court until as recently as 1979 when it moved to Coleford. Floodlit at night, the gaol is paradoxically (considering its original function) among the Forest's most beautiful buildings. It was built in 1792 in accordance with the progressive ideas of Sir George Onesiphorus Paul (1746–1820) who, after a misspent youth, had become high sheriff of Gloucestershire. In a 1784 pamphlet he had pointed out that it was, in a manner of speaking, more dangerous being sent to jail than being sentenced to death, three times as many prisoners dying from fevers (mostly typhoid) in Gloucestershire's jails each year than were executed.

The advanced concept for the Littledean bridewell was that it should be a 'house of correction', not merely a place of punishment. It was laid out in two wings providing twelve separate cells for males, twelve for females. Each inmate had a sleeping cell and a day cell up above where they worked at picking hemp or suchlike tasks, and the design sought to maximize fresh air and daylight. The nineteenth century imposed a harsher regime. A treadwheel was introduced, prisoners were assigned more than one to a cell, and while individual WCs were introduced they were later removed. It closed as a prison in 1845 when the advent of the Severnside railway (the South Wales Railway) made it simpler to send offenders to Gloucester jail but it continued as Littledean's police station. Part was converted into the magistrates' court in 1874 when the lease on the Newnham building ran out.

The magistrates were much concerned by the fractious conduct of Forest commoners in the last half of the century, continuing the centuries-old battle against the Forest administrators. Carrying out a 'heyning' (round-up) of stray animals in 1856 the keepers impounded sheep belonging to Thomas Meredith,

The Littledean gaol, with Huntley churchwarden Jim Rollinson of the Ecclesiastical Insurance owners.

William Adams and James Virgo of an extensive Blakeney Hill family. The threesome summonsed the Newnham keeper for illegal incarceration of their animals according to Forest law but took the interim precaution of releasing their beasts from the Newnham pound one night, for which they were fined 5 shillings each. During an 1864 heyning at Drybrook the keeper was attacked by a group who successfully retrieved their horses. At Coalway commoners rescued their pigs from another round-up after throwing stones at the keepers and injuring one of their sons. The duel ended in tragedy in 1895 when the authorities clashed with what became known as the Virgo gang.

In 1893 Walter Virgo was sued by a neighbour after his sheep munched their way through her vegetable garden. The newly installed Deputy Surveyor ordered the rounding up of some of his sheep, which Virgo predictably rescued in a night raid. The nocturnal activities of Walter, his sons and associates were by now so out of hand that the issue was even raised in Parliament. One night a police patrol encountered Aaron and Moses Virgo and attempted to arrest them 'on suspicion'. The Virgos resisted violently, subsequently being sentenced to a month's

Littledean Hill's Royal Foresters and a lunchtime gathering of regulars with landlord Tony Milliner (centre).

imprisonment. A later encounter ended more disastrously when the police accosted three unnamed men who began to insult them and throw stones. One hit Sergeant Morris behind the ear and killed him. But no one was ever convicted of the crime.

The full account is given by Chris Fisher in the most peculiar of any book about the Forest. With the unappealing title of *Custom, Work and Market Capitalism*, it is a Marxist academic study by an Australian miners' union official which, only inside the cover, reveals it is about *The Forest of Dean Colliers, 1788–1888*. He tells a cracking story, nevertheless, which ends with an unexpected denouement – or perhaps not so unexpected in the context of eight centuries of fraught coexistence between Forest officials and 'encroachers'. After a few more years of skirmishing, the Office of Woods in 1898 ordered a survey of Forest sheep. It counted around 10,000 belonging to 236 owners, 190 of whom owned less than than 50 each. The Commissioners announced it was a very serious problem and something would have to be done about it. In the event they tacitly agreed that nothing would be done about it, just so long as the sheep badgers accepted (which they didn't) that their sheep were there on sufferance and should not ideally exceed 5,000. And there, a hundred years later, the matter rests.

From the Littledean junction Broad Street stretches northwards to the foot of Littledean Hill where the old road climbs along the so-called High Street and then up The Ruffit to the corner occupied by the Royal Foresters Hotel. The view from here across the River Severn's meanders over Gloucester towards the Cotswolds is among the most stunning vistas anywhere in Britain. On a weekday lunchtime the place is unexpectedly crowded. Foursomes of retired folk are playing dominoes, pints of cider on the table in front of them. Many were former colliers, each with a fascinating story to tell – except their accents were almost impenetrable. 'You have to be a Forester in a Forest pub,' agrees landlord Tony Milliner, who took over the pub six years ago and is chairman of the Forest of Dean Licensed Victuallers Association. 'You have to be able to understand their ways.'

He and fellow LVA landlords were alarmed that after decades of continuing closures of pubs, present circumstances threatened the continued existence of those clinging on in the Forest towns and villages. 'The brewers are too greedy,' he suggests. 'The more trade you get, the more they try and take out of you. They are cutting their own throats.' As proprietor of a free house he could choose his suppliers but many of his LVA colleagues were less fortunate. At Yorkley's Nag's Head landlady Myra Byatt laughs when you ask the reason for so many pubs disappearing. 'Lack of trade!' she says. 'When brewery companies are asking between £160 and £300 a week rent it's hardly surprising small houses can't make a profit.'

Notices pinned on the walls of her pub announce details of forthcoming cricket fixtures, darts and skittle team games, and various charity events, all contributing towards the village's existence as a community. She counts off pubs in the vicinity which have already closed: the George, the Crown and the Stag. Of her own place she says: 'We nowadays get more youngsters coming in – the older ones can't afford to get out so much these days.' Her description is supported by Roger Barnett, LVA secretary, who took on Bream's Rising Sun (now the Village Inn) in 1989 and Whitecroft's Miners Arms in 1991. Of the latter he says, 'I'd been there two years when it was put up for sale and sold to one of the new pub holding companies. A village used to have the church, the school and the pub, and they all used to help each other. When the pub goes the community spirit dies.'

Peter, a long-time customer in the corner, comments, 'In thirty years we had three landlords here. In the past three years we've had thirty.' Yet the pub survives because of its skittle alley, used by two men's and two women's teams each week, and good lunchtime food for staff from Whitecroft's cluster of modern factories. For most evenings, though, Peter is less sanguine. 'In the old days everyone had the attitude, let's have a bit of fun. When the piano got going everyone had to sing – even if they couldn't sing! Someone ought to record the old songs before they pass away.'

❖ ❖ ❖

Trying to arrange a meeting with the Forest of Dean Morris Men after one of their winter Wednesday evening practice sessions at Ruardean's Malt Shovel, it was upsetting to learn they had been barred. It wasn't for the first time, either.

The Malt Shovel, Ruardean, origin of the Horlicks drinks empire, with local historian (and district and parish councillor) Andrew Gardiner and new owner Mark Drew.

Soon after forming in 1968 at Coleford's Old White Hart, then base of the Forest's folk music club, the landlord threw them out. In the 1970s Coalway's Britannia Inn asked if they would kindly leave. In the 1980s Joyford's Jovial Colliers wished them a long goodbye. In the 1990s Newnham's The Club suggested a relocation. The problem was not their behaviour but that their practice rooms were in skittle alleys which in Forest pubs are often on the first floor above the main bar. Their jumping up and down and hitting the floor with sticks tended to cause structural readjustments in the ceilings beneath.

Their departure from the Malt Shovel wasn't insisted upon by proprietor Mark Drew but was at their own suggestion. Having bought the sprawling building when Whitbread put it up for auction after it had been closed a couple of years, Mark had spent a small fortune on doing it up. A restaurant had been added at the back with kitchen to match, smart bedrooms had been fitted in upstairs, and the bar area had been opened up to display the newly discovered open fireplace and well. For the Malt Shovel is among the most ancient of public houses, tradition claiming that it is as old as the church. While the present structure is not quite as old as that, it retains features from medieval times such as its flagstone floors and well, and windows in the upper storeys from Elizabethan times.

Its large size, a surprise in a village today off the beaten track, is less surprising when you imagine the importance of the old route across the Forest from Drybrook down to the Wye. Today's main road veers down towards the valley at the village centre but in the old days continued past the Malt Shovel and down the lane which now peters out before reaching Lower Lydbrook. While a centre of mining and iron smelting from Norman times, with workers' settlements creating the Ruardean Hill and Ruardean Woodside hamlets up the twisting tracks towards 'the highest point of Dean', it was outside the statutory Forest and thus had its own manor house, early church and serious pub.

Many pubs in the old days brewed their own beer weekly. The Malt Shovel, as its present name suggests, had a larger malthouse serving other local pubs as well as its own requirements. The foundations of the old brewhouse sheds can be seen around it, as well as the small granary. It was here that the Horlicks milk drink fortune was created. The long-established Horlick family lived opposite. Two brothers, William and James (1844–1921), survived the ailments which killed six children who would have been their aunts and uncles, some of the deaths possibly caused by unpasteurized milk. The brothers set about trying to devise a means of making milk powder on a back kitchen boiler, using a bain-marie copper flask already there for the beer mashing process. Failing to produce a marketable product, they sailed to America where James gained sufficient investment to crack the problem. Already rich by 1906, he returned to build his British factory alongside the Great Western Railway at Slough, was awarded a baronetcy in 1914, and installed himself in the Cowley manor outside Gloucester, from where he contributed towards good causes in his home village.

This saga of local boy makes good, probably the most dramatic of any in the Forest's history, is told by Ruardean-born Andrew Gardiner (sixty-one). Parish councillor for more than thirty years, governor of the village school for almost as long, and elected a district and county councillor as an Independent two years ago, Andrew is a cornucopia of information about the village's history. Sitting in front of the Malt Shovel fire I ask why he hasn't written it all down. He explains he has been working for several years on compiling an oral history of the Glosters' experiences in the Korean War. His brother had been one of those captured there and suffered terrible experiences in prisoner-of-war camp before being released. He was hoping to publish it to mark the war's fiftieth anniversary in 2001.

In the comfortable surroundings of the Malt Shovel bar one was reluctant to raise the question of who killed the bears. In the wrong company the question was liable to provoke old antagonisms. Andrew was able to explain, however, that the notorious incident happened when a travelling troupe of Frenchmen brought their two dancing bears to Cinderford in 1889. This caused offence to the town's rowdier elements following rumours of a child's death somehow related to the animals. The Frenchmen sought to escape but were pursued to Ruardean where the Cinderford (and, some say, Drybrook) hooligans did the unfortunate animals to death.

Selected Further Reading

Anstis, Ralph. *Warren James and the Dean Forest Riots* (Albion House, 1986)
——. *The Industrial Teagues and the Forest of Dean* (Alan Sutton Publishing, 1990)
——. *The Diary of a Working Man 1872–1873: Bill Williams in the Forest of Dean*, edited by Bess and Ralph Anstis (Alan Sutton Publishing, 1994)
——. *Four Personalities from the Forest of Dean* (Albion House, 1996)
——. *Man of Iron – Man of Steel: The lives of David and Robert Mushet* (Albion House, 1997)
Beech, Mabel. *Wye Valley & Forest of Dean* (Thornhill Press, 1994)
Bent, Maurice. *The Last Deep Mine of Dean* (M.V. Bent, 1988).
——. *The Musical Tradition of Dean* (M.V. Bent, 1997)
Bright, Thomas. *The Rise of Nonconformity in the Forest of Dean* (Forest of Dean Newspapers, 1954).
Cockburn, Jack. *Staunton* (1996)
Elrington, C.R. (ed) *A History of the County of Gloucester – Volume X: Westbury and Whitstone Hundreds, including Newnham, Tidenham and Westbury-on-Severn* (Oxford University Press, 1972)
Field, Graham. *A Look Back at Norchard* (1978)
Fisher, Chris. *Custom, Work and Market Capitalism: The Forest of Dean Colliers, 1788–1888* (Croom Helm, 1981)
Foley, Winifred. *A Child in the Forest* (BBC, 1974)
——. *No Pipe Dreams for Father* (Futura, 1977)
——. *Back to the Forest* (Macdonald & Co., 1981)
——. *The Forest Trilogy* (Oxford University Press, 1992)
Hart, Cyril. *The Extent and Boundaries of the Forest of Dean and Hundred of St Briavels* (John Bellows, 1947)
——. *The Verderers and Speech-Court of the Forest of Dean* (John Bellows, 1950)
——. *The Commoners of Dean Forest* (British Publishing Co., 1951)
——. *Laws of Dean* (British Publishing Co., 1952)
——. *The Free Miners of the Royal Forest of Dean and Hundred of St Briavels* (British Publishing Co., 1953)
——. *Lord Bledisloe, of Lydney* (Forest of Dean Newspapers, 1957)
——. *'101 Not Out': The Story of Lydney Cricket Club* (Forest of Dean Newspapers, 1963)
——. *Watts of Lydney* (Forest of Dean Newspapers, 1965)
——. *Royal Forest: A History of Dean's Woods as Producers of Timber* (Oxford University Press, 1966)
——. *Practical Forestry for the Agent and Surveyor* (Estates Gazette, 1967); 3rd Edition (Alan Sutton Publishing, 1991); reprinted (1995 and 1998)
——. *Archaeology in Dean: A Tribute to Dr C. Scott-Garrett, MBE* (John Bellows, 1967)
——. *The Industrial History of Dean* (David & Charles, 1971)
——. *The Verderers and Forest Laws of Dean* (David & Charles, 1971)
——. *British Trees in Colour* (Michael Joseph, 1974); paperback (Michael Joseph for Mermaid Books, 1986)
——. *Coleford: The History of a West Gloucestershire Forest Town* (Alan Sutton Publishing, 1983)
——. *Taxation of Woodlands* (1986)
——. *The Regard of the Forest of Dene in 1282* (D.A.P. Publishing, 1987)
——. *The Forest of Dean – New History 1550–1818* (Alan Sutton Publishing, 1995)

Herbert, N.M. (ed) *A History of the County of Gloucester – Volume V: Bledisloe Hundred, St Briavels Hundred, The Forest of Dean* (Oxford University Press, 1996)

Lawrence, George. *Kindling the Flame – 150 Years of Methodism in the Forest of Dean, 1824–1974* (Forest of Dean Newspapers, 1974)

Nicholls, H.G. *The Forest of Dean* (John Murray, 1863)

——. *The Personalities of the Forest of Dean* (John Murray, 1863)

——. *Iron-Making in the Olden Times* (1866)

——. *Nicholl's Forest of Dean* (David & Charles, 1966)

Paar, H.W. *The Severn and Wye Railway* (David & Charles, 1963)

——. *The Great Western Railway in Dean* (David & Charles, 1965)

Phelps, Humphrey. *Just Around the Corner* (Thornhill Press, 1974)

——. *Just Across the Fields* (Michael Joseph, 1976); paperback (Sphere, 1978)

——. *Just Over Yonder* (Michael Joseph, 1977)

——. *Just Where We Belong* (Michael Joseph, 1978)

——. *The Forest of Dean* (Alan Sutton Publishing, 1982)

——. *Uncle George and Company* (Alan Sutton Publishing, 1984); paperback (1987)

——. *The Forest of Dean in Old Photographs* (Alan Sutton Publishing, 1983)

——. *The Forest of Dean in Wartime* (Alan Sutton Publishing, 1995)

——. *Forest Voices* (Sutton Publishing, 1996)

Potter, Dennis. *The Changing Forest* (Secker & Warburg, 1962); (Minerva, 1996)

Walters, Bryan. *Ancient Dean and the Wye Valley* (Thornhill Press, 1992)

Wakins, Baden. *The Story of Flaxley Abbey* (1985)

Index

Addison, Revd David 56
Aldridge, Ron 18
Aldridge, Geoff 19
Allen, Ray 106
Angel Hotel, Coleford 104
Anstis, Ralph 92
Aston, George 3

Baber, Frank & Margaret 25
Baglin, Lyndon 68
Balsdon, Revd Derek 62
Baptists 61
Barnett, Roger 11
Bathursts 95
Beech, Mabel 86
Belfry, Littledean 107
Bell, R.A.J. 85
Bent, Maurice 70
Blaisdon Hall 99
Bledisloes *see* Bathursts
Bolter, Pat 46
Boevey, Catharina (1670–1726) 94
Brambell, Dr James 30
Bramer, Harry 98
Bright, Thomas 85

Campbell, Sir James, Deputy Surveyor, 1854–93 3
Camilleri, Edward 59
Cardale, Dr John 30
Carson, Dr Charles 30
Chappell, Cecil 66
Christopher, John and Sheila 97
Cinderford Swanbrook Band 67

Clearwell Castle 98
Cotterill, Eileen and John 90
Crawley-Boeveys 94
Crawshay, Edwin and William 99

Davies, Revd Cliff 58
Davies, Ernest 15
Davies, Phil 38
Dean Forest Railway 37
Dean Heritage Centre 40
Denton, Jack and Norma 43
Dilke, Sir Charles, MP, 1892–1911 102
Drew, Mark 111
Drybrook Male Voice Choir 69

Emery, Professor John 31
Evans, Hubert and Winifred 69
Everard, John 1

Flaxley Abbey 91
Flintham, Revd John 63
Foley, Winifred 52
Forest of Dean Male Voice Choir 68
Forest of Dean Young People's Band 66

Gage, Laurie 42
Gardiner, Andrew 112
Gordon-Smith, George 33
Grindle, Harry 45
Grindle, Percy and Roy 43

Harris, John 37
Hart, Cyril 84
Harvey, John 13

Herbert, Nicholas 88
Hooper, Dr Arthur 29
Horlick, James (1844–1921) 112
Howard, Brian 68
Howell, Albert 10

James, John 59
James, Warren 105
Johns, Brian 87
Johnson, Revd Gordon 48
Joiner, John 41
Jones, June 69
Juriča, John 89

Kear, Bernard 74
Kear, Harry 101

Lambert, Marina 69
Latham, Joyce 76
Lawrence, Revd George 85
Lewis, Phyllis 54
Littledean Hall 97
Lydney Lydmet Band 65
Lydney Park 94

Machen, Edward, Deputy Surveyor,
    1808–54 6
McLean, Douglas 51
Malt Shovel, Ruardean 111
Mahony, Brian 5
Marfell, Gill and Wally 72
Methodists 62
Milliner, Tony 110
Miners Arms, Whitecroft 111
Moravians 61
Morgan, Becky 69
Morgan, Keith 48
Morgan, Robert 67
Morgan, Robin 9
Mountjoy, Timothy (1824–96) 102
Mullin, Sr Jan 61
Mushet, David 8
    Robert 84

Nag's Head, Yorkley 110
Nelmes, Kate 69

Nicholls, Revd Henry ix

Oakes, Tim 24
Olivey, Elsie 86

Paar, H.W. 87
Parker, Bill 38
Parkhouse, Neil 87
Paul, Sir George Onesiphorus (1746–1820)
    108
Pinkerton, Revd Patricia 59
Peterken, George 8
Piggott, Roy 14
Phelps, Dougie and Geoff 37
Phelps, Humphrey 78
Pope, Alec 40
Pope, Ian 87
Powell, John 86
Pritchard, Eric 6
Proctor, Ivan 7
Prosser, Ray 17
Pyrkes 97

Radley, Eric 64
Rees, Mike 35
Royal Foresters, Littledean Hill 110

St Briavels Castle 90
Sanzen-Baker, Reginald, Deputy Surveyor,
    1954–68 2
Speech House 101
Standing, Ian 41
Swinley, Bill 20

Tandy, Dr Bill 52
Taylor, Andrew 79
Teague, James 82
    Moses 69
Tremlett, April and John 26

United Reformed Church 63

Venner, Bart 79
Virgo gang 109

Walkerdine, Robert 68

Walters, Bryan 86
Watkins, Baden 93
Watts, Arthur and John 42
Watts, Melville 31
White, Brian and Kevin 65
Willett, Revds Andrew and Sally 63

Winter, Sir John (1602–*c*. 85) 95
Woodward, George and Lynn 22
Wright, Ray 11

Yeates, Des 65